# CATHOLIC
# HIPSTER:
## *The Next Level*

"Tommy Tighe takes hipster Catholicism up a notch with *Catholic Hipster: The Next Level*. From refocusing on the Sabbath to blessing houses, this book is a reminder that there is so much we can do to get closer to God. If you are looking to find God in deeper and more meaningful ways, this is your guide."

**Christopher Wesley**
Author of *Rebuilding Youth Ministry*

"In *Catholic Hipster: The Next Level*, Tommy Tighe and fellow writers fire up Catholics about living out their faith in a way that's passionate and authentically *them*. This book belongs on the shelf of any Catholic longing to live out the quirky sides of their personality while embracing Jesus, justice, and the Church."

**Claire Swinarski**
Author of *Girl, Arise!* and creator of *The Catholic Feminist* podcast

"Whether you identify with the word 'hipster' or not, this compilation of essays from a variety of young Catholics who live their faith boldly and creatively will encourage you in your faith. Find tips on everything from praying the Rosary to observing Ember Days to reading J. R. R. Tolkien. This book has something for everyone."

**Sr. Theresa Aletheia Noble, F.S.P.**
Author of *Remember Your Death*

"Your Catholic faith is cooler—and weirder—than you have been led to believe. Tommy Tighe is the perfect person to guide you through the goldmine of our hipster heritage and offer practical, down-to-earth examples on how to implement it in your daily life."

**Zac Davis**
Associate Editor at America Media and cohost of the podcast *Jesuitical*

"Tommy Tighe returns with a wealth of information about Catholicism's hidden gems that will surprise, provoke, edify, and challenge readers to reconsider what they think they already know about the Church. From the weekly Mass-goer who has never, ever skipped a single holy day of obligation to a seeker curious to learn more about this ancient faith, *Catholic Hipster: The Next Level* has something for everyone."

**Michael J. O'Loughlin**
Author of *The Tweetable Pope*

# CATHOLIC HIPSTER:
## *The Next Level*

How Some Awesomely Obscure Stuff
Helps Us Live Our Faith with Passion

## TOMMY TIGHE

AVE MARIA PRESS **AVE** Notre Dame, Indiana

*To Karen, James, Paul, Andy, and Charlie. Your love
inspires me to keep going, and I just know our sweet
Luke is looking down on us and smiling.*

Unless otherwise noted, scripture quotations are from *New Revised Standard Version Bible*, copyright © 1989 National Council of the Churches of Christ in the United States of America. Used by permission. All rights reserved.

# CONTENTS

# INTRODUCTION

## Tommy Tighe

Welcome!

If you read the original *Catholic Hipster Handbook*, you know the deal: we're here to bring you *everything* cool about being authentically Catholic in today's increasingly secular culture.

If this is your first time delving headfirst into the world of hipster Catholicism, get ready!

What you hold in your hands is the *second* journey through the Catholic faith and how to genuinely live that faith out loud in the world. How can we effectively grow in our relationship with Christ and his Church? How can we excel in sharing the Good News with all those we meet, all those so badly in need of that good news these days? How can we embrace the Catholic faith and live it in a way that shows the world exactly how cool it is to be Catholic?

That's what this book is all about!

Do you find yourself quietly chanting the Sanctus in Latin, even though the cantor is leading the congregation in English? Do you kneel to receive Communion in the place where the altar rail used to be in the hopes your witness will lead to the rail being reinstalled? Are you signed up for four different days each week at your parish's Perpetual Adoration chapel and devastated that your parish priest wasn't able to fit your home blessing into his busy schedule until July?!

If so, this book is for you.

Are you looking for ways to bring your passion for social justice into everything you eat and drink? Are you curious about the best way to form a community around you and wonder if J. R. R. Tolkien might have the answer? Or perhaps considering getting a tattoo and wondering not only if it would be okay but also how it might actually glorify the Lord?

If so, this book is definitely for you!

Last time around, we focused on rediscovering the Catholic faith: getting back in touch with the attitude, the stuff, the life, and the attraction. Now we're taking our love of Catholicism to the next level! *Catholic Hipster: The Next Level* is all about living our Catholic faith and living it with *passion*.

Join a whole batch of incredible contributors set to show you how to honor the Lord's Day in style, hit the road for a pilgrimage in honor of everyone's favorite American Catholic author, live a life marked with a radical hospitality only seen in days past, and so much more. We're also bringing a fresh batch of cool saints and forgotten prayers to spark your spirituality in new and exciting ways. From St. Catherine of Bologna to St. Nicholas of Tolentino to St. Antonio Maria Pucci, these saints will equip you with a new clique ready to intercede on your behalf. From the Suscipe, to the *Sub tuum praesidium*, to the Dedication of a Family or Community, a whole new group of prayers will help you grow closer to Our Lord and those around you.

We've got everything you need to learn, grow, and, most importantly, live the Catholic faith right here, right now. We're ready to take you along for the ride. If you're up for it, leeeeeeeet's gooooooo!

# Part 1
# LIVING WITH FAITH

## Tommy Tighe

When someone rediscovers the Catholic faith, it's a joyous moment, to be sure. Whether the person was a cradle Catholic who strayed away during college (yours truly) or a convert who studied his or her way into the truth of the Catholic Church thanks to the early Church Fathers, there's a party in heaven when someone comes back into the fold.

But, there's also a nagging question that comes up for everyone: now what?

How are we supposed to take the beautiful truths of our faith and put them into action? We know that our lives are supposed to be radically changed by Jesus, but how? We know that others will "know we are Christians by our love," but what does that even mean?

Oftentimes, we can feel stuck at square one, wishing there were detailed instructions for how to live the faith *in today's world*.

Well, buckle your seat belts, boys and girls: you are about to embark on the very instruction manual you've been praying for!

How can we pause the noise and find God in the silence? How should we open ourselves up to the Holy Spirit and the gifts he has waiting for us? What are some of the go-to devotions and spiritual practices that can help kick-start our walk with the Lord? Are we seriously considering joining a religious order?!

All of these questions, and many more, will be answered ahead. Are you ready?

# HONOR THE SABBATH: LEARNING TO PAUSE THE NOISE IN OUR LIVES TO HEAR GOD

Sr. Brittany Harrison, F.M.A.

One of the high school theology courses I teach is "World Religions." The purpose of this course is to blend cultural education with an understanding of how religious faith shapes the experience, perspective, and values of people. Without discounting the role of Jesus Christ as the sole mediator between God and man, our Redeemer and the font of mercy, we can identify in the major world religions how elements of truth, beauty, and goodness can be found in most traditions and are points of commonality for beginning conversations and invitations to learn more about Christianity.

I find that the dedication with which so many Muslims perform *salah,* the daily prayers that begin at dawn and mark time until night, as well as the Buddhists' emphasis on the gift and peace found by dwelling in the present moment, to be good reminders about how religion should be not simply a once-a-week affair but a life-transforming aspect of who we are.

What I struggle with the most, as a symptom of our busy, overcommitted, productivity-focused culture, is "honoring the Sabbath." Number three on a list of ten commandments that God entrusted to Moses, "remember to keep holy the Sabbath," is a directive I try to keep, but I often forget what it means. In studying the Jewish faith, I have discovered among more conservative followers a very beautiful tradition of keeping the Sabbath with great intentionality and preparing for it with joy. In some traditions, the Sabbath is referred to as the "Sabbath Queen" and is ushered in by the women of the family by lighting candles at the moment it begins as they entrust to God their deepest prayers.

Some forms of Judaism forbid anything that even hints at work on the Sabbath, including kindling fires (which includes starting car engines and turning on light switches) and carrying things (such as pocket change). Although I find that approach to be a bit extreme for my situation, this dedication to observe the Sabbath as a serious, holy, and joyful reminder that human value does not come from work, that family time is important, and that God is worthy challenges me to examine how I make my weekly Sabbath different from the other six days of the week.

I have to be honest: sometimes my Sabbath day looks like every other day. I spend it as a "catch up" day with my grading and lesson plans and spend very little time "resting in the Lord" and dedicating time to simply enjoying the gift of life. When I don't carve time out each Sabbath for extra prayer, extra time with others, and extra rest, I feel it during the following week. God knew what he was doing when he told us to keep the Sabbath holy, because doing so leads us to be more whole.

Perhaps the most distracting element of modern life can include the pressure to keep up on social media, answer never-ending emails, and respond instantly to text messages. I have found peace and renewal by going social media–free on Sundays and going for walks without a cell phone in my pocket. I am a member of the Salesian Sisters, and it is our tradition to make a holy hour together on Sundays, pray midday prayer from the Divine Office, and have an extra-special dinner. We "waste" extra time at the dinner table, sharing with one another and enjoying one another's presence.

The Sabbath is a gift we too often fail to open. How each of us lives it will be tailored to our individual personalities and needs. If we want to be countercultural and give a prophetic message to our world, let us join our Jewish brothers and sisters by observing the Sabbath as a reminder that God is above all and that our value comes from being children of God, not from our paychecks and accomplishments. God knew that we needed this day of rest and renewal, so why not accept the gift that he offers?

## COOL SAINT
## ST. MARIA DOMENICA MAZZARELLO

The foundress of the Salesian Sisters, St. Maria Domenica Mazzarello had a very cool name. Her name literally translates from Italian to "St. Mary Sunday." Anyone who has spent time in Italy can attest to the fact that it's very hard to find open businesses on the Sabbath day in smaller villages that still keep to the Italian tradition of honoring Sundays by greater rest and family time. St. Maria Domenica made sure that her sisters and the young people boarding at Salesian schools treated Sundays as wonderful days for celebration with dressier clothing, better food, fun games, and some added rest. Everyone looked forward to Sundays. May we learn from the example of "St. Mary Sunday"!

## FORGOTTEN PRAYER
## JESUS, YOU ARE THE
## LORD OF THE SABBATH

Jesus, you are the Lord of the Sabbath. By rising on the third day, you sanctified Sundays as a reminder of your presence and victorious love. Help us to detach ourselves from our productivity-focused culture and to spend each Sabbath as a day of connecting more deeply with you and our loved ones. Remind us that our value comes from your infinite love, not from what we accomplish and how much we do. Amen.

## LIVING THE FAITH

What are some simple ways you can make Sundays different from every other day of the week? What pressures can you remove for twenty-four hours? What activities can you participate in with your loved ones where you are truly present with one another? Whether it's a special meal, a shared movie, an opportunity to go somewhere new, or a chance to just sit around and swap stories, Sundays are a chance to reconnect to life. Commit to make your next four Sundays different and see how it transforms your week.

# HEALING THE SICK AND RAISING THE DEAD: JUST YOUR AVERAGE CATHOLIC HIPSTER

Jackie Francois Angel

My good friend St. Paul once raised a young man from the dead (who, by the way, fell out a third-story window after falling asleep during Paul's sermon that went "on and on" [Acts 20:9, NABRE]). My friend St. Peter would walk around, and people would try just to get in his shadow so they could be healed (Acts 5:15–16). Two thousand years later, my friend Andrew prayed at baggage claim in an airport for an atheist woman's foot to be healed in the name of Jesus, and she came to believe after her chronic foot pain disappeared. My friend Fr. Neil is an exorcist who has a gift of discernment of spirits and knows when people "are experiencing demonic oppression." My friend Sr. Miriam has prophetic dreams and *twice* has told me that she had a dream of me being pregnant when no one else besides my husband knew that I was, in fact, pregnant! (She even had the due date right on the last kid.) St. Padre Pio, my big brother in Christ who lived last century, would bilocate and read hearts. Another brother in Christ who lives today, Patrick, gets words of knowledge from God to encourage others in the Body of Christ.

What's crazy is that this is not at all crazy for the disciple of Jesus Christ. Jesus himself said that those who believe in him will be accompanied by signs and wonders such as casting out demons, speaking new languages, and laying hands on the sick and healing them (see Mark 16:17–18). The hipster Catholic who loves the Church Fathers knows that the early Church was rife with miracles, signs, and wonders so that people would come to know Jesus and that the Body of Christ would be encouraged. As time passed, heresies about the body ensued (such as "spirit = good, body = bad"), and the Enlightenment emphasized reason and denigrated faith. The average Catholic kind of expected that the charisms of the Holy Spirit were just meant for the "holy people" or the "saints," while others with a suspicion of the miraculous or charisms would burn people at the stake.

But current hipster Catholics, whether preferring the Extraordinary Form or *Novus Ordo*, have seen that God's response to today's post-Christian culture is a resurgence in signs and wonders. When the vast majority of people won't listen to reason, God's response is miracles. St. Paul talks about the charisms we receive through baptism in 1 Corinthians 12, and the *Catechism of the Catholic Church* expresses that, "whether extraordinary or simple and humble, the charisms are graces of the Holy Spirit which directly or indirectly benefit the Church, ordered as they are to her building up, to the good of men, and to the needs of the world. Charisms are to be accepted with gratitude by the person who receives them and by all members of the Church as well" (799–801).

So if you're a hipster and you still aren't quite sure what charisms you have received in Baptism, sit down with scripture in one hand (opened to 1 Corinthians 12) and a foamy latte in the other, and ask for the Holy Spirit to be stirred up in your life and for God to show you which charisms he wants you to use to encourage and build up the Body of Christ in faith, hope, and love!

## COOL SAINT
## ST. IRENAEUS

St. Irenaeus (ca. AD 115–202) was a third-generation Christian who as a boy learned the Gospel from St. Polycarp, who first heard it from the apostle John. Signs and wonders were everyday aspects of the early Church and expected from those who were baptized Christians. He said about them,

> Those who are truly the Lord's disciples . . . perform [miracles] in his name for the well-being of others, according to the gift that each one has received from him. For some truly drive out devils, so that those who have been cleansed from evil spirits frequently believe and join the Church. Others have foreknowledge of things to come: they see visions, and utter prophecies. Still others heal the sick by laying their hands on them, and they are made whole. Yes, forever, the dead have even been raised up, and remained among us for many years. And what more shall I say? It is not possible to name the number of the gifts that the Church throughout the whole world has received from God, in the name of Jesus Christ who was crucified under Pontius Pilate, and which she exercises day by day for the benefit of the Gentiles. (*Against Heresies*, 2.32.4)

## FORGOTTEN PRAYER
## COME, HOLY SPIRIT!

Come, Holy Spirit! Fill the hearts of Thy faithful, and enkindle in them the fire of Thy love. Let us pray. Grant, O merciful Father, that Thy Divine Spirit may enlighten, inflame and purify us, that He may penetrate us with His heavenly dew and make us fruitful in good works, through Our Lord Jesus Christ, Thy Son, Who with Thee, in the unity of the same Spirit, liveth and reigneth, one God, forever and ever.

## LIVING THE FAITH

When people ask you to pray for them, don't just pray for them "later." Pray for them right then and there. If someone is hurting or sick, pray in the name of Jesus for his or her healing. If God can use a donkey (see Numbers 22:22–35), God can use you! He can do anything he wants, so don't be afraid to step out in faith and ask for God to heal someone's body, heart, mind, or soul! If you prayed over one hundred people in a wheelchair to walk, and only one of them did, would you still pray over the one hundred? Of course! Be bold and ask for the saints to intercede and pray with you.

# JESUS, I TRUST IN YOU (EASIER SAID THAN DONE)

Katie Prejean McGrady

There's no easy way to say this, so I'll just say it: you are not meant to be in control of your own life. Hate to break it to you, but it's true.

Sure, the world has convinced us that we're supposed to plan out every moment of every day, we're supposed to strive for temporal successes in the form of material wealth and goods, we're destined for power and might and strength and retweets, and the only way to get all those things is to be in control. But the truth is, when we're in control of ourselves and our destinies, we tend to really mess things up.

St. Maria Faustina Kowalska, born in northern Poland in 1905 as Helena, learned this "I'm not supposed to be in control" thing the hard way.

Helena had a strong desire to join a convent at just seven years old, and for years she longed for the day she could become a religious sister. But her parents, strict and hardworking and very poor, insisted she become a housekeeper instead. Devoted to her parents, Helena obeyed their request but struggled greatly with this deep longing to become a bride of Christ. She longed to control her own destiny—to go when she wanted and where she wanted—but she was made to wait.

In 1924, at nineteen years old, Helena had her first vision of Jesus, who told her to leave at once to join a convent. With no instructions other than to head to Warsaw, she left.

Every time I hear this story—a young girl who worked as a housekeeper saw Jesus and he told her to go to the big city to join a convent—I'm shocked. What courage that must have taken! What boldness! What trust in the Lord! But when she got to Warsaw, with this command from Jesus and love for his Church, Helena was turned away from every single convent she approached until one said she could join if she could buy her own habit.

Imagine: you are told by Jesus to join a convent, and no convent will take you, so you have to keep working as a housekeeper—the very job that reminds you of being told no to fulfilling your vocation years before—so that you *can* join and fulfill the Lord's request of you. I don't know about you, but that's the point where I'd just look at Jesus and say, "Sorry, buddy, I'm out. Either make it easy, or I ain't doing it." I'd want to take control.

But Helena, soon to be Sr. Maria Faustina of the Blessed Sacrament, didn't give up. She didn't try to control the situation; she simply trusted in Divine Providence, worked as hard as she could, and in 1926, became the religious sister she'd always wanted to be.

Over the years, as she worked as a cook and housekeeper in the convent, she had numerous visions of Jesus, who spoke to her, again and again, as the "King of Divine Mercy." Clad in white, with two rays of light radiating from his chest in red and pale blue, Jesus spoke to Maria Faustina, reiterating a simple yet profound message: I love you, and I want you to trust me. He asked her to have an image painted of him as she saw him, with words at the bottom: Jesus, I trust in you.

Maria Faustina began keeping a diary of her visions of Jesus and the things he said to her. This diary, and devotion to the Divine Mercy image, tells the story of a young religious sister swept up in a beautiful relationship with the Lord who spoke to her heart, longed for her devotion, and wanted her to engender passionate devotion to the image of Divine Mercy. In a diary entry on September 13,

1935, Sr. Maria Faustina shared a vision of the Chaplet of Divine Mercy—a series of prayers to be prayed on rosary beads to obtain mercy, to trust in Christ's mercy, and to show mercy to others. Simple, short, easy to remember and even easier to pray, this Chaplet of Divine Mercy is now one of the most popular devotions of Catholics around the world, most traditionally prayed in novena form (nine straight days of prayer) beginning on Good Friday and ending the Sunday after Easter, Divine Mercy Sunday.

Ultimately, the Chaplet of Divine Mercy, the image of Divine Mercy, and the story of St. Maria Faustina Kowalska are about trusting the Lord rather than trying to remain in control: trusting what he says, trusting what he asks of us, and trusting his providential and divine plan, which is one of great goodness, endless gifts, and merciful love.

## COOL SAINT
## BL. MICHAEL SOPOCKO

The story of St. Maria Faustina Kowalska can't be told without making mention of her spiritual director and biggest supporter, Bl. Michael Sopocko. A priest and professor in Vilnius, Lithuania, where Maria Faustina eventually settled, he greatly supported her as she shared about her visions, and he encouraged her to keep the now-famous diary of her experiences and encounters with Jesus.

Bl. Sopocko delivered the first sermon about the Divine Mercy on April 26, 1935, and, two days later, was the first priest ever to display the image on the first Sunday after Easter, now Divine Mercy Sunday. A year later, he wrote the first brochure explaining this simple yet profound devotion, placing the image of the Divine Mercy on the front for all to see. St. Maria Faustina said of him, "This priest is a great soul who is completely filled with God," and she credited his efforts in sharing this devotion to the Divine Mercy to the salvation of countless souls.

## FORGOTTEN PRAYER
## THE LITANY OF TRUST
## BY THE SISTERS OF LIFE

The Divine Mercy Chaplet is popular and widespread. But Sr. Faustina Maria Pia, a Sister of Life, has written a beautiful and lovely litany that makes reference to the well-known Divine Mercy devotion and challenges us for modern times. Here's part of that litany; you can find the full litany at www.sistersoflife.org/litany-of-trust.

> From the belief that
> I have to earn your love
> **Deliver me, Jesus.**
> From the fear that I am unlovable
> **Deliver me, Jesus.**
> From the false security
> that I have what it takes
> **Deliver me, Jesus.**
> From the fear that trusting you
> will leave me more destitute
> **Deliver me, Jesus.**

## LIVING THE FAITH

Do a "month of trust" in which every day you pray the Divine Mercy chaplet, pray the Litany of Trust, or read a few pages from St. Faustina's diary.

# OBSERVING EMBER DAYS

Haley Stewart

Have you heard of observing the Ember Days of prayer and fasting that come around four times a year? It's become clear that the Church needs more acts of reparation, and laypeople and religious alike are reaching out for penitential traditions. Since my friends on Catholic Twitter were tweeting about Ember Days and a former professor and fellow parishioner put together an email series about them, I guess I got peer-pressured into observing them this year. And, as we all know, the best kind of peer pressure is Ember Day peer pressure.

While observing these days of penitence is now optional, it's an option worth taking. The Ember Days are three days of prayer and fasting (a Wednesday, Friday, and Saturday) that come around four times a year, and they originate from very ancient Christian fasting traditions. The early Christians fasted on Wednesdays (the day Jesus was betrayed) and Fridays (the day of the Crucifixion), but Ember Days are also informed by Old Testament Jewish fasting traditions. Each trio of days culminated on a Saturday (when Christ was entombed) with a Mass, and it was a traditional day for new priests to be ordained.

Coinciding with the changing of the seasons and agricultural life, Ember Days were the original Catholic connection to the rhythm of God's creation before that concept went all mainstream in the encyclical about care for our common home, *Laudato Si'*. Observing Ember Days orients us to a spirit of gratitude for the bounty of the earth. There's the Michaelmas Embertide (Michaelmas after the Feast of St. Michael on September 29), Advent Embertide, Lenten Embertide, and Whit Embertide ("Whit" after "Whitsunday," another name for Pentecost). And because everybody loves a traditional mnemonic device, to remember when Ember Days occur just think "Lenty, Penty, Crucy, Lucy" (because they are close to Lent, Pentecost, Feast of the Holy Cross, and Feast of St. Lucy, respectively).

Observing Ember Days means fasting (eating one meal and two snacks) on Wednesdays and Saturdays and fasting and abstaining from meat on Fridays of Embertide. (If you want to get technical, those two snacks on Wednesdays should not include meat, but the meal can include it.) According to *The Golden Legend*, a medieval religious text by Jacobus da Voragine, this fasting is meant to dry up our vices so that the herbs of virtue can grow. You can think of them as a quarterly mini-retreat and opportunity for an examination of conscience and penance in pursuit of holiness. Feeling overwhelmed with twelve extra days of fasting? Just remember that Catholics used to have fifty-two days of fasting a year! We can handle Ember Days, fam.

## COOL SAINT
## ST. GWEN TEIRBRON

St. Gwen was a sixth-century Welsh saint and daughter of the king of Brittany whose firstborn became St. Cadfan. After being widowed, she married St. Fracan and had more saintly children. She was called Teirbron or "triple-breasted" because she had children from two marriages, but some artistic depictions portray her with three breasts. People started to feel weird about this, so many of her icons and statues were buried (or maybe stored in dusty parish attics). Breastfeeding mothers would ask for her intercession. According to legend, she was captured by pirates who chopped two of her fingers off with an axe before she escaped by climbing over the side of boat and walking across the English Channel. Her relics are believed to be in the church of Whitchurch-Canonicorum in Dorset where a St. White is buried ("Gwen" means "white") and where axes and ship motifs in the church may refer to her adventure with the pirates.

## FORGOTTEN PRAYER
## COLLECT ON EMBER WEDNESDAY IN SEPTEMBER

May our frailty cease, we beseech Thee, O Lord,
by the remedies of Thy mercy:
that what is being ruined by its own condition
may be repaired by Thy clemency.
Through our Lord.

## LIVING THE FAITH

Follow the traditional fast and go to Mass on Wednesdays, Fridays, and Saturdays of each Embertide for a year. See if you can convince your priest to encourage your parish family to observe them together!

# FIRST MASS,
# LAST MASS, ONLY MASS

Julie Lai

In 2017, a third-party content analysis study was done on Catholic Twitter users on what seemed to be the most pressing issues facing Catholics today. The results were as follows: the song "On Eagle's Wings," the cross clap, and holding hands during the Our Father. The researcher concluded that these issues have put a divisive stress on the Church. It has pitted father against son and son against father, mother against daughter and daughter against mother. One Catholic Twitter user, @thatonecatholicgirl, said, "Like you know, um, with such problems, every Catholic seems to be wondering, like, how will the Church overcome such times?"

Okay, okay, yes, you got me; this isn't true. ("On Eagle's Wings" is mildly infuriating, though.) Jokes aside, if I sat down with you and asked what one issue you think is the most problematic for the Church, I'm sure you'd have a laundry list of possible responses. In my view, the biggest issue plaguing the Church right now is our life-draining apathy. And Catholic hipsters have the opportunity to change that.

As Catholics, we have the most astonishing, earthshaking, heavenly gift: the Eucharist, and yet we're apathetic to it. We go to Mass like little children being dragged to the dentist by obligation.

We count down the minutes as if we're waiting for recess. And the minute Mass is over, we avoid eye contact with people whom we say Christ is in (unless they're cute). If a non-Catholic walked into your local church, would that person really believe the Eucharist is the source and summit of our faith?

We have a call to reawaken and reclaim the reality of the Mass. We are called to look at the Lord with new eyes of love. We are called to be drawn into the mystery.

## COOL SAINT
## VENERABLE FRANCIS-XAVIER NGUYỄN VĂN THUẬN

Venerable Văn Thuận is not quite a saint yet, but he's on his way. You can thank me later when you tell all your friends on his canonization day, "Yeah so, I knew Francis-Xavier Nguyễn Văn Thuận before he was cool."

Fr. Văn Thuận was brilliant. He had an intimate and contagious devotion to the Lord. Shortly after becoming a bishop in 1967, Văn Thuận was captured by North Vietnam's army and was imprisoned for his faith by the communist government.

Bishop Văn Thuận was taken into prison empty-handed, yet he still found ways to celebrate Mass. In prison, he was able to ask for necessities so he wrote home and asked for "wine for his stomach pains"; in response, his family sent wine and some tiny, broken-up hosts. Every day in the darkest hours of the night, he celebrated Mass with three drops of wine and tiny hosts in the palm of his hand and snuck the Body and Blood of Christ to six other prisoners. After Mass, he used cigarette papers to protect the remaining hosts, and the prisoners took turns adoring the Lord. The love of Christ in this forbidden church community was contagious. Buddhists and non-Christians were converted. The prison had to keep changing prison guards because they kept converting.

Each of us has a "prison" that can keep us from going to Mass or diving into the Mass: our lack of time, our distractions, our sin, our lack of motivation, our anger at the Church, our children, our work, and more. And sometimes we can only offer the Lord our weakest yes. And that's okay. All that Bishop Văn Thuận could offer was the tiniest drop of wine, but the Lord took that and turned it into the Blood of Christ. Surely, he can do much with our littlest offerings too.

## FORGOTTEN PRAYER
## MOTHER TERESA'S PRAYER FOR PRIESTS

Mother Teresa said to a group of priests: "Celebrate this Mass as if it is your first Mass, your last Mass and your only Mass." Her challenge is a call for us too. Pray these words before Mass starts, centering yourself to become present to the liturgy.

## LIVING THE FAITH

### CELEBRATE MASS AS IF IT IS YOUR FIRST MASS

Imagine what it might be like if you were an adult going to Mass for the first time. Would you get there early as you're not quite sure what to expect? Would you be a little nervous and uncomfortable about "doing the right thing"? Would you take in the whole church, examining the art and the people? Would you start to become curious about certain parts of the Mass? Would you desire to meet people after Mass? Imagining such questions can help us look at the Mass with new eyes of love. It could lead us to want to read and learn more about the meanings of certain parts of the Mass. (For a deeper understanding of the Mass, read Scott Hahn's *The Lamb's Supper* or Mark Hart's *Behold the Mystery*.)

### CELEBRATE MASS AS IF IT IS YOUR LAST MASS

Mass for the first Christians was everything but convenient or comfortable. If a person was going to Mass, it very well could have been his or her first, last, and only Mass. The first Christians went to Mass knowing that the consequence for going could be death.

They went to Mass not knowing when the next Mass would be or if there was going to even be another Mass in their hometown. Ask yourself, How can I come into Mass more intentionally?

## CELEBRATE MASS AS IF IT IS YOUR ONLY MASS

If I could only go to one Mass for my entire life, I'd hang onto every single moment. I'd fight to be exactly where my feet were, even if my mind tried to lead me otherwise. I'd review the readings before Mass and read a reflection on them. I'd journal the homily so I could stay present to what the priest was saying and remember it forever. I would worship with every fiber of my being. Ask yourself, If I could only go to one Mass in my life, how would I experience that Mass?

# THIRD ORDERS: EXTREME HIPSTER CATHOLICISM

## Holly Vaughan

A big part of hipster Catholicism is preserving the ancient traditions of the Church and bringing them into the modern world. Hipster Catholics love age-old prayers, Latin Masses, sacramentals, and being thoroughly and unabashedly Catholic. We are also drawn to monasteries, convents, and archabbeys, whether it be by vocation or just to visit. This is only natural, of course, since these places also strive to carefully preserve the traditions of our faith and live them to the fullest.

Anyone who has visited the monks or the sisters for Daily Mass or the Liturgy of the Hours knows the beauty of their devout liturgy, not to mention the comforting peace that envelopes one just from spending time in these holy places. Many a monk or sister has found his or her vocation this way. But what about those of us who are drawn to the life and charism of the monastery but have already discerned that our vocation does not lie in religious life? Must we be content to watch from the sidelines?

Absolutely not! Our Church, good mother that she is, provides for the needs of all of her children. Religious orders know of this desire of the laity to experience monastic life and have known of it for a long time. They also know that their faith and charisms need to get out into the world and make a difference even in places where the monks and sisters are not readily able to be present. They want their work to travel far beyond the monastery walls and reach as many people as possible. Enter: Third Orders, also known as Lay Orders.

Third Orders are laypeople who live their lives in the world as they always have but who incorporate the values and charisms of the order they choose to join. They are a real part of the religious family—they learn and study and even go through a novitiate period—but instead of living at the monastery, they take what they learn and carry it with them into the world by living it in their everyday lives. In most cases they make promises—some orders renew annually, some make lifetime promises once the novitiate is over—which should still be discerned and taken seriously but are not vows like religious take.

Different Third Orders have different commitments they ask of their members, but most pray at least Morning and Evening Prayer of the Liturgy of the Hours daily. This connects members spiritually to their monastic family (and the Universal Church!) as they pray the same prayers the monastics are praying. Often the commitments depend on the charism of the order. I am a Benedictine oblate. Benedictines are asked to pray the Liturgy of the Hours as stated above and to try to do lectio divina every day. The motto of the Benedictines is *Ora et labora* or "Pray and work." Benedictines consider the Liturgy of the Hours as "the work of God," and we offer up our normal work of the day as a prayer as well. Our charism centers on prayer, hospitality, balance, and moderation. Other orders have different commitments; for example, Dominicans are very dedicated to the Rosary (it is said that the Rosary in its current form was given to St. Dominic by Our Lady) and ask their Third Order to pray it daily, in addition to the Liturgy of the Hours.

How about a quick rundown of Third Orders? Maybe you will find that God is calling you to a certain religious family! Here are the main ones, and some basic information about each.

- **Benedictine Oblates:** Oblates are a part of the whole order of Benedictines but are also connected to a particular "house," be it a monastery, convent, or archabbey. Their charisms are centered on prayer, hospitality, moderation, and balance. Benedictines are called to pray, to love and welcome people, and to care for the world that God has given us. A well-known member is Servant of God Dorothy Day.
- **Dominicans:** Like Benedictines, Lay Dominicans incorporate the charism of the Dominican Order into their lives in the world: prayer, study, and preaching. The Dominican Order is known as the Order of Preachers. The vowed religious and the lay members study the Word of God and preach it by their lives and by their words. A well-known member is St. Catherine of Siena.
- **Franciscans:** This order lives a simple lifestyle based on the life of St. Francis. The five main points pulled from their Rule are (1) love God, (2) love one's neighbor, (3) turn away from sinful tendencies, (4) "receive the Body and Blood of our Lord Jesus Christ," and, as a result of the above, (5) produce worthy fruits of penance—a renewed life characterized by charity, forgiveness, and compassion toward others. A well-known member is St. Joan of Arc.
- **Carmelites:** The charism of the Carmelites is based on contemplative prayer. As a part of the Third Order, living in the world, Lay Carmelites find a balance of contemplative prayer and taking the fruits of that prayer out into the world. A well-known member is honorary member St. John Paul II.

## COOL SAINT
## ST. MEINRAD

St. Meinrad was a Benedictine monk. He is the patron saint of hospitality. At the end of his life he was living in a small hermitage when two men set out to find his hermitage and kill him. St. Meinrad was offering the Mass as they approached, and sensing what was about to happen, he finished the Mass, kissed the relics of the saints that he possessed, and commended his coming agony to the Lord. He then went out and greeted his soon-to-be murderers, expressed his sorrow that they had arrived too late to attend his Mass, gave them bread and clothing, and instructed them to do what they had come to do. His only request was that they leave a lit candle burning at each end of his body. After they had killed Meinrad, they placed a candle at his head and took the other candle to go light it. When they returned, the unlit candle they had left was burning brightly. Overcome by fear, they fled the humble hermitage but were overtaken by ravens that made their crime known to the townspeople. St. Meinrad's abbott and brothers came for his body and buried it with honor, and this little man who welcomed his own murderers has since become known as the Martyr of Hospitality.

## FORGOTTEN PRAYER
## PRAYER IN HONOR OF ST. MEINRAD

O God, you are made glorious in the
martyrdom of the hermit Meinrad.
Through his intercession,
help me to grow in my love for you
and in devotion to the Blessed Virgin Mary.
May I follow his example in Christlike
hospitality and in single-hearted prayer.
Through Christ our Lord. Amen.

## LIVING THE FAITH

Visit a monastery! Even if you don't feel that you are called to Third Orders, a day at a monastery is refreshing and spiritually fortifying. If you are interested in Third Orders, research the different orders and their charisms, and be open to the call of God. He may be waiting to introduce you to a whole new spiritual family!

# THERE'S MORE THAN ONE WAY TO PRAY A ROSARY

Tommy Tighe

As a Catholic, Mary is kind of my jam.

Whenever I need to call in the reinforcements to help me storm heaven, she's my go-to mediatrix. And while I can completely conceptualize in my head that Mary is a human being just like me, in my heart I can feel like she's so far out of my league that there's no way she would be able to understand what I'm going through in my day-to-day life, especially as a parent. That's why, while the Rosary has brought me untold amounts of comfort in times of intense suffering, it has also left me feeling even further away from Mary at times.

Thankfully, as a Catholic hipster constantly on the lookout for the awesomely obscure in our faith, I stumbled upon an alternative contemplative prayer that completely changed things for me and was just what I needed: the Servite Rosary, or the Rosary of the Seven Sorrows.

This Rosary originated with the Servite Order and focuses on the Seven Sorrows (or *Dolors*, if you want to impress your friends) of the Blessed Virgin Mary. The journey you embark upon as you move the beads through your fingers goes a long way toward bringing the Holy Mother of God right up beside you and into your life.

27

## THE FIRST SORROW: THE PROPHECY OF SIMEON

Just days after the birth of my first son, he had an extremely rough night that culminated in our rushing him to our doctor. Once there, we were given the crushing news that he would be admitted to the hospital and kept overnight for observations. It was terrifying to hear.

The Bible doesn't document any of Jesus' battles with childhood illness, but Mary was told by Simeon that her baby boy "is destined for the falling and the rising of many in Israel" (Lk 2:34) and that her own heart would be sword-pierced with sorrow over him. She knows a parent's fears.

## THE SECOND SORROW: THE FLIGHT INTO EGYPT

Do you know those times when you find yourself feeling left out in the cold, either literally or emotionally? Where you've felt unwelcome, even among your closest friends and family, simply because you're tracking in a different direction? Mary's definitely been there—unmoored and with only the consolation of God, her husband, and her son to take comfort in.

## THE THIRD SORROW: THE LOSS OF THE CHILD JESUS IN THE TEMPLE

Think of the wave of stomach-churning, dizzying terror that you feel when you lose track of your child, even for a minute while out in public, and the emptiness and guilt that inevitably replace your panic once you find him or her. You may only have lost sight of your child for a moment, but the self-recrimination lives on: "How could I have been so distracted?" Mary has been there, in spades.

## THE FOURTH SORROW: THE MEETING OF JESUS AND MARY ON THE WAY OF THE CROSS

As a mental health professional, I have given support to parents as they have faced their struggling children, have realized their children still haven't hit rock bottom and still aren't ready to get the help that is needed, and have been forced to let them go, to let them fall the rest of the way, in hopes that they will finally rise.

That confrontation is awful, because feeling helpless in the face of your child's trouble is terrifying and heartbreaking. There is nothing worse. Mary knows what it means to stand helplessly before the pain in her child's eyes. There is no better companion in such terrible moments as these.

## THE FIFTH SORROW: THE CRUCIFIXION

Have you ever had to experience the unbearable and unspeakable pain of losing a child to death, to estrangement, or because a child has lost his or her way in life? Mary's right there, crying alongside you.

## THE SIXTH SORROW: THE TAKING DOWN OF THE BODY OF JESUS

We all have that day: the day of darkest suffering—when we must see something and bear it, and it makes us feel like we just can't go on—a day of nothing but pain, and a future that seems empty and void. Mary, once handed her bloodied, broken son, understands.

## THE SEVENTH SORROW: THE BURIAL OF JESUS

We all know how this story ends: "But take courage; I have conquered the world!" (Jn 16:33). Jesus wins, yes. And yet we mostly forget it; we continually second-guess whether a happy ending could ever be on its way. Deaths, financial worries, miscarriages, marital problems, work difficulties—hope can be hard to find in these difficult moments, and we want to give up.

Mary must have felt this way as she stood by and watched her Son be placed in a borrowed tomb. Whether or not she knew at that moment that Easter was on the way, she certainly understands how difficult it can be for our hearts to see beyond Good Friday.

With good reason, Mary can seem so far above us as to seem out of reach, but if we take a moment to reflect upon all she endured throughout her life, we start to see how fully she understands everything we're enduring throughout ours. The Servite Rosary has helped me to see this, clearly, and to believe that if I hang on, Mary will gladly take me by the hand and lead me the rest of the way home.

### COOL SAINT
## ST. ANTONIO MARIA PUCCI

Born in 1819, the second of seven children, Antonio felt called to life in a religious order as a child but faced opposition from his father. He eventually pushed through this opposition and joined the Servite Order in 1837, and he was ordained to the priesthood six years later. He served as pastor of a small parish for forty years, and he became well known for taking care of the poor and sick of the area. He was canonized by St. John XXIII in 1962.

St. Antonio Maria Pucci, pray for us.

### FORGOTTEN PRAYER
## CLOSING PRAYER FROM THE SEVEN SORROWS ROSARY

Let intercession be made for us, we beseech Thee, O Lord Jesus Christ, now and at the hour of our death, before the throne of Thy mercy, by the Blessed Virgin Mary, Thy Mother, whose most holy soul was pierced by a sword of sorrow in the hour of Thy bitter Passion. Through Thee, Jesus Christ, Savior of the world, Who with the Father and the Holy Ghost lives and reigns, world without end. Amen.

## LIVING THE FAITH

Contemplate the sorrows of Our Lady and all she endured. Pick up a Servite rosary (or count away on your fingers, if you can't get your hands on one) and walk alongside Mary as she pushed through her trials with faith in God's plan. Think about the sorrows you have faced in your own life and how Mary, through her own sorrows, deeply understands what you're going through.

When you realize the Mother of God understands you, you can take a deep breath and find the courage to continue on.

# THE SONG OF SONGS: THE MASS IN THE OLD TESTAMENT

## Patrick Neve

At Franciscan University, there were three Mass times a day, which at first sounded like a blessing but ended up being a curse on my Catholic guilt. You see, two Masses were in the middle of the day, which meant I frequently had something going on. The other Mass was before anyone had anything to do that day. It was at 6:30 a.m.

A Mass that early in the morning was good for discipline and a great way to start my day. However, I found it was hard to pay attention and remain prayerful because 6:30 Mass had no music. Because of this, I am now of the opinion that if the music minister's voice isn't awake, I shouldn't be either.

My friend Nino and I were talking about this after Mass one morning, and he said that when there is no music accompanying the Mass, he meditates on the Song of Songs, particularly the springtime song in Song of Songs 2:8–16. That day we had a long conversation about that passage and how it relates to the Mass. Below, I split the passage up into seven sections so you can use the Song of Songs to meditate on the Mass.

| SONG OF SONGS | PART OF MASS |
|---|---|
| The voice of my beloved!<br>Look, he comes,<br>leaping upon the mountains,<br>bounding over<br>the hills. . . . | **INTRODUCTORY**<br><br>Start off Mass by remembering why you are there. You are there because you heard the voice of God. Remember that voice throughout Mass today. |
| Look, there he stands<br>behind our wall,<br>gazing in at the windows,<br>looking through<br>the lattice. | **READINGS**<br><br>Christ peers out at us through the scriptures. He is hidden in the Old and preached in the New. Look for your beloved in the scriptures being read. |
| My beloved speaks and says<br>to me:<br>"Arise, my love, my fair one,<br>and come away;<br>for now the winter is past,<br>the rain is over and gone.<br>The flowers appear on<br>the earth,<br>the time of singing<br>has come,<br>and the voice of<br>the turtledove<br>is heard in our land. | **GOSPEL**<br><br>The Gospel is where the Lord speaks to us plainly. In all he does and says, he is saying these words to us: the winter of death has past; the springtime of the Resurrection is here.<br><br>How is this Gospel calling you to live in the Resurrection? |

| SONG OF SONGS | PART OF MASS |
|---|---|
| "The fig tree puts forth its figs,<br>and the vines are in blossom;<br>they give forth fragrance.<br>Arise, my love, my fair one,<br>and come away. | **PREPARATION OF THE GIFTS**<br><br>At this point, we know what is coming. We can smell the fragrance of the wine being brought. It reminds us of Christ in the Eucharist. We hear the voice of God more clearly now as he calls us to communion.<br><br>What fragrance do we put forth? Does our fragrance remind others of Christ? |
| "O my dove, in the clefts of the rock,<br>in the covert of the cliff,<br>let me see your face,<br>let me hear your voice,<br>for your voice is sweet,<br>and your face is lovely. | **CONSECRATION**<br><br>Are these Christ's words to you or yours to him? If you feel in love with Jesus, say them at the elevation. If you feel nothing, let him say them to you. |
| "Catch us the foxes,<br>the little foxes,<br>that spoil the vineyards—<br>for our vineyards are in blossom." | **BEFORE RECEIVING**<br><br>As you say "Lord I am not worthy," ask him to help you empty your heart of anything that does not belong to him. |

| SONG OF SONGS | PART OF MASS |
|---|---|
| My beloved is mine and I am his. | AFTER RECEIVING<br><br>In the Eucharist, you have become one with Christ. You belong to him and he belongs to you. Whatever the Lord is doing in your heart this week, let him. Ask how you can help.<br><br>Repeat this verse to yourself if you find yourself becoming distracted. |

The Song of Songs ends with the two lovers in anticipation of the wedding feast. This Mass is what they were waiting for, and it is right at our fingertips. We are able to live in the springtime the two lovers dreamed about.

## COOL SAINT
## ST. GREGORY OF NAREK

St. Gregory of Narek was a tenth-century Armenian monk. His prayers and writings focused on how he could offer himself up to God. The Church in Armenia's relationship with the Church in Rome is long and complicated, but in 1996, Pope John Paul II and the head of the Armenian Church signed a declaration of mutual faith. This led to St. Gregory of Narek being declared a Doctor of the Church in 2015 by Pope Francis.

## FORGOTTEN PRAYER
## FROM *SPEAKING WITH GOD FROM THE DEPTHS OF THE HEART* BY ST. GREGORY OF NAREK

The voice of a sighing heart, its sobs and mournful cries,
I offer up to you, O Seer of Secrets,
placing the fruits of my wavering mind
as a savory sacrifice on the fire of my grieving soul
to be delivered to you in the censer of my will.

Compassionate Lord, breathe in
this offering and look more favorably on it
than upon a more sumptuous sacrifice
offered with rich smoke. Please find
this simple string of words acceptable.
Do not turn in disdain.

May this unsolicited gift reach you,
this sacrifice of words
from the deep mystery-filled chamber
of my feelings, consumed in flames
fueled by whatever grace I may have within me.

## LIVING THE FAITH

Go to a Mass without music and use the Song of Songs to remain prayerful.

# J. R. R. TOLKIEN: CATHOLIC HIPSTER

Kaitlyn Facista

You've probably heard of J. R. R. Tolkien, the author of beloved classics such as *The Hobbit* and The Lord of the Rings series (and if you haven't, it's time you did). Since the publication of *The Hobbit* in 1937, millions of readers around the world have journeyed through Tolkien's Middle-earth on epic adventures alongside his endearing halflings. But what you may not have heard is that John Ronald Reuel Tolkien himself was a devout Catholic, and The Lord of the Rings is, in his own words, "a fundamentally religious and Catholic work."

Tolkien was born in 1892 to Arthur and Mabel Tolkien, the oldest of two boys. When Arthur passed away just three years later, Mabel and her sons moved to Birmingham, England, to be closer to her family. Tolkien and his brother, Hilary, had a happy childhood; already Tolkien was learning Latin and botany and beginning to create his own languages. However, everything changed in 1900, when Mabel and her sons were received into the Roman Catholic Church. Their conversion was met with staunch disapproval by Mabel's Protestant family, and without her family's financial and emotional support and despite Mabel's tireless work to provide for her family, they soon found themselves in the depths of poverty.

Mabel passed away only four years later. Tolkien himself noted the correlation between his mother's early death and her family's disapproval of her conversion, seeing her as a martyr for her faith.

After their mother's death, Tolkien and Hilary were, for the most part, brought up by Fr. Francis Morgan, a local priest. Fr. Francis cared greatly for the boys' spiritual well-being and ensured they were immersed in the faith their mother so deeply believed in. By this time, Tolkien had grown into a remarkable linguist and lover of great literature, becoming proficient in Latin and Greek as well as inventing languages of his own. And under the care of Fr. Francis, he grew in love and understanding of the Catholic faith.

After earning his first degree from Oxford in 1915, Tolkien enlisted in the British army and married his childhood love, Edith Bratt, shortly before being posted to France. He fought in Battle of the Somme, one of the bloodiest battles in human history, and struggled through illness and injury for the remainder of the First World War. Yet through it all, he continued to write in his spare moments. In 1925, Tolkien returned to Oxford as a professor of Anglo-Saxon, where he would spend the remainder of his professional career. He and Edith were married for more than fifty years and raised four children together.

Though he had composed bits and pieces of his own mythology throughout his youth, it was at Oxford that Tolkien's vision of Middle-earth finally began to take shape. He wrote the first line of *The Hobbit* when a sudden inspiration struck while grading papers, and the tales of Middle-earth continued to grow until his death in 1973. There are no churches or practiced religions in Middle-earth, and you won't be introduced to any thinly veiled religious allegories in his works. Instead, when you read The Lord of the Rings, you'll find yourself immersed in an imaginary world that somehow begins to feel more real than our own because it was inspired by the truths of our Catholic faith.

Woven throughout the life of J. R. R. Tolkien are two common threads: a profound love for the Catholic faith and a remarkable passion for language and literature. Tolkien admits that many elements of his stories, while not formally allegorical, resemble aspects of our own world and hold Catholic truths that can be applied to our lives. His stories highlight the great struggle of good versus evil, echoing the Christian story of salvation. He coined the term *eucatastrophe* to describe a sudden, unexpected happy turn when all hope is lost. It is through eucatastrophe that Middle-earth is ultimately saved, and it's worth noting that Tolkien referred to Christ's Resurrection as the greatest eucatastrophe of all. Tolkien presents themes such as mortality, heroism, friendship, sacrifice, humility, courage, and power in a way that holds up a mirror to our own lives. Within the peoples of Middle-earth—men, dwarves, elves, hobbits, wizards, orcs even—we see ourselves, even if only a little. This is true of all good literature, I think, but Tolkien's world is unique in both its depth and its Catholicism.

Just as there are many lessons to be learned from Tolkien's Middle-earth, there are many lessons we can learn from his life as well. From an early age, he recognized his passions and pursued them wholeheartedly. His love for language led him to invent several of his own as well as become an esteemed teacher of philology; his love for mythology led him to create his own world and entire legendarium to go with it. He didn't settle for mediocrity, and neither should we.

Tolkien didn't set out to evangelize via story; he simply set out to tell a story. But because he himself was so immersed in his faith, his Catholic worldview shone through in an incredibly powerful way. The Lord of the Rings doesn't need to lean on Catholicism as a crutch; instead, it can stand on its own as a well-written work of literature. Encouraged by Tolkien's example, we should pursue our passions wholeheartedly, confident that when we are rooted in our faith others will see it.

Since Tolkien's death, a love for him has continued to spread around the world. His stories have inspired countless readers, planting the seeds of truth, beauty, and goodness in their hearts as they read. May we all be encouraged by his life, his work, and his faith to set out upon our own adventures with the same devotion, humility, and courage of the peoples of Middle-earth.

J. R. R. Tolkien was the kind of man you'd find at a non-costume party fully dressed up as a polar bear on a Saturday night and then at Mass the following morning, loudly responding in Latin despite the post–Second Vatican Council liturgy. His life was rich with laughter and friendship, steadfast faith and dedication, and a deep love for story. That sounds like a pretty exemplary Catholic hipster life if you ask me.

## COOL SAINT
## BL. JOHN HENRY NEWMAN

The connection between Bl. John Henry Newman and J. R. R. Tolkien serves as a neat reminder of the way our lives can have a lasting impact for generations to come. After the death of their mother, Tolkien and his brother were cared for by Fr. Francis Xavier Morgan. Fr. Morgan was a priest of the Birmingham Oratory, which had, in 1848, been founded by Bl. John Henry Newman. So if it weren't for Newman's conversion and work within the Church, Mabel Tolkien might not have ever met Fr. Francis, and without him her sons might not have been brought up with a faith as strong as they were.

John Henry Newman was born in 1801 in London. He was an Anglican priest for about twenty years before converting to Catholicism in 1845, and he was ordained a Catholic priest after two years and was later made a cardinal. Much like Mabel Tolkien, Newman suffered a great loss of friendships and faced many hardships because of his conversion. He was an influential writer, theologian, and preacher. Newman was beatified in 2008 by Pope Benedict XVI.

Bl. John Henry Newman, pray for us!

## FORGOTTEN PRAYER
## *SUB TUUM PRAESIDIUM*
## ("BENEATH THY PROTECTION")

This prayer is often prayed as a prelude to the Litany of the Blessed Virgin Mary (also known as the Litany of Loreto). Tolkien had such a strong devotion to Mary that he actually translated this prayer from Latin into Quenya (one of the Elvish languages he created). I'll just give you the English version, though: "We fly to thy patronage, O holy Mother of God; despise not our petitions in our necessities, but deliver us always from all dangers, O glorious and blessed Virgin."

## LIVING THE FAITH

If you've never read anything by J. R. R. Tolkien before, grab a copy of *The Hobbit* or The Lord of the Rings books next time you're at your local library or used bookstore. They're classic stories and should be required reading for all Catholic hipsters, even if fantasy isn't your preferred genre. Because Tolkien was so steeped in his Catholic faith, the truth and beauty of the Gospel have been poured out into the very fibers of Middle-earth. So just do it. It's good for your soul. But also, you never know when you'll be able to use Middle-earth as an opportunity to introduce the Gospel to someone who might otherwise be resistant to the Catholic faith or religion in general.

# GUITARS AND ORGANS

## Matthew Sewell

As a young Catholic, on fire for the Lord and his Church, I find myself in a conundrum every now and then. Despite my love for the organ-playing, full choir-singing, symphony-brass-accompanying parish I attend on a near-daily basis, I also harbor a great affinity for more, shall we say, contemporary liturgical ditties.

Those by Catholic superstars Matt Maher and Audrey Assad top the list (most among the young, hip Catholic crowd would understand), but I may or may not also swoon over the likes of Jesuit Bob Dufford's "Be Not Afraid," David Haas's "You Are Mine," and—*gasp!*—even on occasion, Michael Joncas's funeral classic, "On Eagle's Wings."

Granted, the affection for some of those Oregon Catholic Press classics is nothing more than nostalgia. If I had a dollar for every time I played "On Eagle's Wings" for a funeral Mass at my home parish, I'd have about seventeen dollars—not much money, but it *was* a lot of "On Eagle's Wings."

Plus, in any discussion on the doctrinal truth (or lack thereof) in certain songs, I'll be the first to say loudly, "No, Mr. Dan Schutte, we do *not* build the City of God . . ." or "Pardon me, Sydney Carter, but I'd wager that the Lord wasn't doing much dancing when he was *on the Cross* . . ." But I nevertheless owe much in my three decades of existence to both styles of worship music, and believe both have much to offer the Body of Christ. St. Paul speaks to what I mean in his first letter to the Thessalonians: "Do not quench the Spirit. Do not despise the words of prophets, but test everything; hold fast to what is good; abstain from every form of evil" (5:19–21).

I'm sure the great apostle did not anticipate those lines being applied to snappy modern hymns—ones easily mistaken as show tunes—but alas. If nothing else, the kernel of truth to be found in every created thing in this world is a significant enough reason to not cast aside cheesy '70s "liturgical" music altogether.

Most of us Catholic hipsters have been raised in parishes where the music selection (and perhaps the musical talent itself) was found wanting. It's admittedly hard to pray with a tone-deaf cantor belting "Gather Us In" while being accompanied by a cheap guitar and a rainstick. But a person striving to raise his or her soul heavenward is equally thwarted by the organist who doesn't know how to work the volume knob.

When it comes to music many would deem as unfit for worship—as with anything else in living the Catholic faith—we're called upon to look outside of ourselves, to seek first the Lord in all things, and to use our reason to identify what's true, good, and beautiful. Only then are we legitimately capable of judging something rightly. The Lord can (and does) work in any milieu, especially ones we find ourselves stuck having to endure; we only need eyes to see and ears to hear. And if nothing else, just do what St. Cecilia did when musicians were playing tawdry songs at her wedding banquet: "Cecilia sang in her heart hymns to Christ, her heavenly bridegroom."[1]

## COOL SAINT
## ST. NICETAS OF REMESIANA

St. Nicetas lived during the fourth and fifth centuries in modern-day Serbia. He's known for being a bishop, a missionary, a musician, and a composer of many Latin hymns. In particular, Nicetas is now thought to be the composer of the ancient Christian hymn of praise, the *Te Deum*, which was for centuries thought to have been written by the great St. Ambrose of Milan. St. Nicetas, pray for us.

### FORGOTTEN PRAYER
## "ADORATION" BY MATT MAHER[2]

Down in adoration falling
This great Sacrament we hail
Over ancient forms departing
Newer rites of grace prevail

### LIVING THE FAITH

Next time you find yourself being serenaded in Mass by a mid-twentieth-century classic, focus not on the tune but on the lyrics to the song. Think critically about what they're saying, even if the notes themselves strike you as that of a thousand nails scraping a chalkboard. If we believe the Lord strives to speak to us in each moment, what is it that he's telling you right then?

Granted, it may well be that he's saying, "This is heretical garbage. Sing a new song in your heart to me until this craziness is over." *But*, if we're open to hearing it, the Lord might just be saying, "Be not afraid. I go before you always. Come, follow me, and I will give you rest."

# DECK THE HALLS WITH WEIRD OLD TESTAMENT ORNAMENTS, FA LA LA LA LA, LA LA LA LA

## Katie Prejean McGrady

Catholicism is old. Like, more than 2,000 years, started by Jesus, ever-ancient old. And while it *is* the most hipster religion, it is not the oldest, and it finds its roots in Judaism and the Old Testament.

So it shouldn't surprise any of us that during Advent, the liturgical season when we deck the halls and prepare our hearts for the arrival of Jesus and the celebration of the greatest moment in human history (the Incarnation), we should also want to remind ourselves of the roots that run deep in our Catholic heritage and tradition. Having a Jesse Tree keeps us connected to our ancient roots and gives us the chance to relive the story of salvation history, walking through each moment that eventually led us to the arrival of sweet little baby Jesus, lying in a manger in Bethlehem.

Jesse, the father of King David, is referenced in Isaiah's prophecy about the Messiah who would one day come to save the world: "A shoot shall come out from the stump of Jesse, and a branch shall grow out of his roots" (Is 11:1). A descendant of King David and thus a descendent of Jesse, Jesus is that "new growth" coming from the roots, and so when we adorn a Christmas tree with illustrated ornaments that remind us of prophets, people, and significant events that led to the birth of Jesus, we are rooting ourselves (no pun intended) in the ancient, beautiful, sometimes confusing, but always life-giving history of our faith.

Each day of Advent, an ornament is placed upon the tree and a story from scripture is read—everything from the well-known story of Adam and Eve (the ornament could have the image of an apple tree) to the story of Hezekiah in Second Kings (the ornament could show an empty tent), each day we're reminded of a moment that built up and led to the arrival of the Messiah, Jesus.

Honoring the Jesse Tree can be as simple or involved as you choose to make it. Some families just read the scripture passage associated with each day, hearing the story of a moment in the Old Testament that foreshadowed and prepared the way for Christ. Some families make handmade ornaments, painting each image as they learn about the reason for a particular symbol; for example, the Friday of the Second Week of Advent we pay attention to Ruth, a woman who stayed with Naomi even in times of trouble and continued to work in the fields and who was given the gift of plenty of grain from Boaz, a landowner who was moved by her story of faithfulness.

The stories in the Old Testament are not irrelevant to us, and each image on a Jesse Tree is a profound reminder of God's providence and love, culminating in the Incarnation, the Word becoming flesh and dwelling among us. Keeping, decorating, and praying with a Jesse Tree during Advent is a visible sign of God's plan, both then and now. It is a tangible reminder of what God has done, does now, and will always do for us: provide, plan, and act on our behalf out of his perfect and abundant love.

## COOL SAINT
## ST. AMBROSE

Bishop of Milan and known as one of the "Great Latin Doctors of the Church," St. Ambrose is best known for being St. Augustine's teacher. Known for his wisdom and understanding of Greek philosophy, Ambrose was converting to Catholicism in 374 when the bishop of Milan suddenly died. The people of Milan gathered at the cathedral to mourn their bishop and wait for the new one to be declared, and a small child cried out "Ambrose for bishop! Ambrose for bishop!" and, while not even baptized, he was named the bishop of Milan. That same day, Ambrose was baptized and confirmed, ordained a deacon and a priest, and installed as bishop.

Ambrose's feast day is December 7, which usually falls in the first week of Advent, when we remember the earliest stories of the Old Testament, namely, the stories of Noah, Abraham, Isaac, and Jacob. Ambrose gave famous teachings on the mysteries revealed in the Old Testament figures, calling attention to the imagery and symbolism of water as foreshadowing the waters of Baptism.

## FORGOTTEN PRAYER
## O COME, O COME, EMMANUEL

O come, O come, Emmanuel, and ransom captive Israel,
That mourns in lonely exile here,
Until the Son of God appear.
Rejoice! Rejoice! Emmanuel! Shall come to thee,
   O Israel.

Amen.

## LIVING THE FAITH

It's super simple to set up a Jesse Tree. Search for "Jesse Tree Ornaments" online, and either make a simple homemade set with construction paper and glue or order a nice set online. Set up your Christmas tree on the first day of Advent, and take some time every day (whenever works best with your schedule) to read the readings for the symbol that day and hang the ornament on your tree. Loyola Press's website has a great Jesse Tree resource.

# LECTIO DIVINA: THE ART OF SACRED READING

## Holly Vaughan

St. Benedict was one of the ultimate Catholic hipsters. He lived in a turbulent time in which civilization was collapsing, and he made radical moves to follow God. Because of his way of life and action he, rather unintentionally, became the father of Western monasticism. When he wrote his Rule while serving as abbot of Monte Cassino, he didn't know its great wisdom would guide monasteries and help shape Western civilization in the twenty-first century (1500 years later!). The Rule of St. Benedict, however, is used by a majority of monasteries today and is also used as a guidebook for parishes, families, and even businesses.

One of the things St. Benedict stressed in his Rule was the importance of a practice called *lectio divina*. Lectio divina (Latin for "divine reading") is a meditative and prayerful way of reading the scriptures that can also be used with any spiritual reading. It is a way to be silent and hear God. Do you ever spend time in prayer waiting to hear God and come away frustrated? Dr. Tim Gray, in his series on lectio divina, reminds us that prayer should be a conversation and that the scriptures can be the key to going from a one-sided monologue to a real dialogue with God.

There are generally four steps to lectio divina: read (*lectio*), reflect (*meditatio*), prayer (*oratio*), and rest (*contemplatio*). Let's take a look at each one of these steps, and see how to read scripture in a whole new way!

The very first thing you have to do is choose a scripture passage to read. This shouldn't be too long, perhaps anywhere from five to fifteen verses depending on the amount of time you have. It could be a favorite Bible story or one of the daily Mass readings; or you could choose a book of the Bible and work your way through it passage by passage, day by day. The choice is yours. Some people also find it very fruitful to journal during the process. If this is something you would like to do, be sure to have a notebook and pen ready.

First up: read (*lectio*). In this step, you simply read slowly through the passage of scripture you have chosen. Gather all the facts; pay attention to any footnotes or commentary included in your Bible so that you read scripture in light of Church teaching. See what word or phrase jumps out at you. Let's take Philippians 4:4–7 for an example: "Rejoice in the Lord always. I shall say it again: rejoice! Your kindness should be known to all. The Lord is near. Have no anxiety at all, but in everything, by prayer and petition, with thanksgiving, make your requests known to God. Then the peace of God that surpasses all understanding will guard your hearts and minds in Christ Jesus" (NABRE).

The footnotes for this passage in my Bible teach that we should rejoice because we know that our Lord, upon his return, will glorify us in both body and soul if we remain faithful. The phrase that jumps out at me when I read this passage through for the first time is "Have no anxiety at all." God may draw you to a different phrase or maybe even only to one word. Whatever word or phrase you are given, take a few minutes (maybe two to three) to reflect on it.

Step two is reflect (*meditatio*). Read the whole passage through again, slowly. While the phrase you have chosen should remain a focus, also be sure to listen to the scripture as a whole. For this step the question to keep in mind is, "What is God saying to me?" Take a little longer this time (three to five minutes), and reflect on this question, listening in the silence of your heart. Remember this isn't a Bible study but a way of interacting with God through his Word.

Next is step three: prayer (*oratio*). Read through the scripture slowly a third time. This is where you respond to God. Respond in prayer to what you hear God telling you through this passage. Be open and honest with God. This is your part of the dialogue. Take close to the same amount of time with this step that you did with step two (three to five minutes).

Step four, rest (*contemplatio*), is really a state of being. Read the scripture through slowly a final time, and then simply rest in the presence of God. Consider an elderly married couple rocking on their porch, content to just be in each other's company. This is an inactive state of simply being present and resting with the Lord. If your mind starts to wander, bring it gently back to the stillness. Contemplation is a gift of God that we are blessed with. Try to spend at least five to ten minutes at this stage.

After you have completed all the steps, end with a prayer of thanksgiving to God for your time together, perhaps the Glory Be prayer. Be patient with yourself as you learn this process, and let it guide you into a deeper relationship with God. Not every step will come easily every time, and that's okay! Persevere, and the fruits will come.

## COOL SAINT
## ST. JEROME

St. Jerome lived in the fourth century and is best known for translating the original Greek and Hebrew texts of the Bible into Latin, which was the language of the people. This translation is known as the Vulgate. Jerome was a fiery type who wasn't afraid of standing his ground. He is sometimes known as one of the crankier saints, but his anger generally only flared when he was defending the faith against heresy. Temper aside, it takes a great love to motivate a man to translate all of the books of scripture by hand. St. Jerome's success at this arduous task makes him a perfect lectio divina saint.

## FORGOTTEN PRAYER
### ORIGEN (AD 184-253)

Lord, inspire me to read your scriptures and to meditate upon them day and night. I beg you to give me real understanding of what I read, that I in turn may put its precepts into practice. Yet, I know that understanding and good intentions are worthless, unless rooted in your graceful love. So I ask that the words of scripture may also be not just signs on a page but channels of grace into my heart. Amen.

## LIVING THE FAITH

Practice lectio divina! It is recommended to practice it daily, but just try it as often as you can with the time you have and build up to a regular schedule. Try it with the daily Mass readings or a favorite passage as mentioned above, but also don't be afraid to add a twist to it—use the practice to read other spiritual books or even to meditate on art, such as a stained glass window that tells a story.

Need a little extra nudge to spend time with the scriptures every day? A partial indulgence was granted by Pope Leo XIII in 1898 to all the faithful who "shall read for at least a quarter of an hour the books of the Sacred Scripture with the veneration due to the Divine Word and as spiritual reading." This indulgence is granted under the usual conditions.

# FASTING: NOT JUST FOR DIETS

Sr. Brittany Harrison, F.M.A.

Intermittent fasting is a very popular way of losing weight. Whenever I scroll through Instagram I am guaranteed to see at least two posts about it, touting the benefits of alternating periods of eating with longer periods of not eating. Many religions integrate fasting into part of their religious practices, such as the month-long sunrise to sunset fast of the Islamic month of Ramadan, to the disciplined fasts of Hindu yogis who seek mastery over their bodies, and the twenty-five-hour repentant fasting of the Jewish solemnity of Yom Kippur.

Christianity is not without its fasting practice, either. Jesus fasted in the desert for forty days and nights (see Matthew 4:1–11), the maximum amount of time a human body can be sustained without food. His fast mirrored the forty years the Hebrews wandered in the desert before entering the Promised Land and the forty days of Noah's Great Flood that purged the earth of sin. Jesus' disciples would have kept the Jewish fasts, as would his mother, Mary, and his foster father, Joseph. In the first gospel written, the Gospel of Mark, Jesus revealed to his disciples the secret to getting rid of particularly troublesome evil spirits: "This kind can go out by nothing, but by prayer and fasting" (Mk 9:28, Douay-Rheims). Fasting became a normal part of the Christian spiritual arsenal, a way of reordering our priorities and focus, of detaching ourselves from whatever form of gluttony we are prone to (a vice that doesn't only apply to food), and of reminding ourselves of the spiritual hunger we should all have for holiness.

St. Basil the Great (330–379), one of the early Church fathers, lauded fasting: "Fasting gives birth to prophets and strengthens the powerful; fasting makes lawgivers wise. Fasting is a good safeguard for the soul, a steadfast companion for the body, a weapon for the valiant, and a gymnasium for athletes. Fasting repels temptations, anoints unto piety; it is the comrade of watchfulness and the artificer of chastity. In war, it fights bravely, in peace it teaches stillness" (Homily on Fasting).

Have I convinced you of fasting's benefit yet? I admit it took me a long time after my conversion to the Catholic faith to finally embrace regular fasting, but once I did, I noticed that fasting made me more reflective, helped me to have greater interior peace, and allowed me to be more attentive to the needs of others. Fasting for me was good medicine against my pride and impatience.

Beginning to fast can seem intimidating, and my best advice to anyone who wants to begin this practice is to start small. If you're a daily coffee drinker, don't suddenly go completely without coffee, but merely drink less. (Being cranky due to a lack of coffee would hardly make for a meritorious fast!) Make sure your intention is in the right place. There is no spiritual profit in fasting just to lose weight or because everyone else is doing it; fasting should be a choice that comes from the heart, to glorify God and declare in a concrete way that only he can truly satisfy us. The physical benefits of fasting may be a nice bonus, but our eyes should be upon Christ when we are fasting, not the bathroom scale.

Not everyone can fast from food or drink, but everyone can fast from something. If you have a health condition, you should talk with your doctor about what is appropriate for you and be prudent regarding your health. If not eating makes you "hangry" (angry or moody because of hunger), going without food might make those around you suffer, so a modified fast of abstaining from your favorite foods may be the best way to offer God a sacrifice.

Some people I know fast from adding condiments in their food (salt, sugar, hot sauce, and so on), or drink only water for a certain number of days, allowing for a very hidden but meaningful fast. If we are creative and honest with ourselves and our spiritual guides about our capacity to fast, we can discern a reasonable form that will help us grow in holiness. Perhaps we find fasting from food or drink to be very easy, but fasting from unkind words, gossip, and judging others to be very hard, so that would be the fast God asks of us. Abstaining from social media, entertainment, and laziness in cleaning the house could be other forms of fasting. Fasting should lead us to be more disciplined, so the best fast we can do is one will require us to grow in that virtue.

When fasting, we have to guard against spiritual pride that may trick us into thinking we are better Christians or more disciplined and holier than those who do not fast. To fast in a way that is pleasing to God, we should do so in discernment with a spiritual guide or friend who knows us well, do it in a humble (and perhaps hidden) way, and do so with simplicity and charity. Often we will be tested when we are fasting. We may be visited by a friend we have not seen in a long time who brings us food they prepared for us. Since the greatest of all virtues is charity, we have to listen to the Holy Spirit in that moment and discern if it would bring more glory to God to eat the treat or to share with that person our decision to fast. Sometimes we must eat the treat and other times we can share our spiritual practice, but never should we impose our spiritual disciplines upon others in an arrogant way by smugly declaring, "I cannot have that as I am *fasting* today." Jesus admonishes us to fast joyfully if we wish to please God: "Whenever you fast, do not look dismal, like the hypocrites, for they disfigure their faces so as to show others that they are fasting. Truly I tell you, they have received their reward. But when you fast, put oil on your head and wash your face, so that your fasting may be seen not by others but by your Father who is in secret; and your Father who sees in secret will reward you" (Mt 6:16–18).

A joyful fast seems like an oxymoron, but when we use the spiritual tool of fasting to reorder our priorities and discipline our desires, we find a freedom that is a fruit of the Holy Spirit's presence and the strength to be more faithful in our *sequela Christi*, the following of Christ.

## COOL SAINT
## ST. MARIA FAUSTINA KOWALSKA

St. Maria Faustina Kowalska—best known for sharing with the world the devotion to Divine Mercy and the image of Jesus with rays of white and red light coming from his heart with the statement, "Jesus, I Trust in You"—frequently employed fasting when praying for special intentions. Because she was a religious sister, her life belonged entirely to God, and God guided her through her superiors in the convent. Consequently, St. Faustina had to ask permission to engage in fasts that were above what the sisters of her congregation normally did. Since her health was delicate, her superiors often wisely moderated her desire to fast from food and drink and assigned her other forms of fasting, such as sacrificing her extra time to help others or giving up a certain kind of food she preferred. She is an example of someone who, in docility to God's direction through her spiritual guides, learned well that what we fast from isn't as important as our intention and humble disposition in fasting.

## FORGOTTEN PRAYER
## PRAYER OF ST. EPHRAIM THE SYRIAN

O Lord and Master of my life!
Take from me the spirit of sloth,
faint-heartedness, lust of power, and idle talk.
But give rather the spirit of chastity,
humility, patience, and love to Thy servant.
Yes, Lord and King! Grant me to see my own errors
and not to judge my brother,
for Thou art blessed unto ages of ages. Amen.

## LIVING THE FAITH

How is God calling you to fast? Spend some time reflecting on this question. Open yourself in prayer to the Holy Spirit and ask him to reveal to you the fast that will help you to grow in holiness. In a journal, or even in the margins of this book, create columns for things, attitudes, activities, and food/drinks that it would be safe, healthy, prudent, and appropriate for you to fast from. The goal is not to make a long list of each but to identify a few and then share them with a friend or spiritual guide who can help you to discern which one or two forms of fasting God is asking you to embrace and for how long. Some people fast every Friday, following the Church's requirement to do penance on Fridays; others fast on Saturdays in honor of Our Lady. Another way to discern the best method of fasting is to reflect upon which sins you frequently bring to the Sacrament of Reconciliation and need help overcoming. Through fasting you can develop "medicine" for that habit of sin. Impatience asks you to fast from sharp words; a lack of charity requires restraining your judgments and speech. If you struggle to be temperate and chaste, creating a form of accountability and weekly fasting can strengthen you in the battle for self-mastery. The simpler and clearer your fasting practice, the more it will help you to grow. When it comes to fasting, starting small and relying upon God's grace to succeed is the shortest path to success.

# Part 2
# LIVING WITH HOPE

## Tommy Tighe

The Church has always had its problems. Or, as a Catholic radio host once put it when speaking with someone interested but unsure about joining the Catholic Church, "Come on in; the water is terrible!"

Despite all the darkness that seems to be circling around our beloved Church and around *us* as we walk through this valley of tears we call life, it can all seem a bit overwhelming. What is the point of all this? Are we really walking along the right path?

We'll be tackling those questions head-on in this section, focusing on the importance of living with hope, or as Jesus put it in the Gospel of John, "In the world you face persecution. But take courage; I have conquered the world!" (16:33).

How does our faith encourage us to engage in fighting for social justice? How can we build community in a culture that is increasingly turning away from personal interaction? How can the Catholic approach to feminism lead us toward a more welcoming, beautiful, and supportive Church? How in the world are we ever supposed to bounce back from a tragedy in our lives where God seemed to be completely absent?

The Catholic faith gives us a hope that can never be taken from us, a hope that can carry us through even the darkest moments. Understanding how to live in that hope is the key.

63

# THEY DON'T CALL US A UNIVERSAL CHURCH FOR NOTHING!

Julie Lai

If we're talking about Catholic hipsterdom, I think we should talk about the most overlooked beauty of the Catholic Church: Her universality. Her diversity.

In the *Joy of the Gospel*, Pope Francis explains that in celebrating diversity, "the Church expresses her genuine catholicity and shows forth the 'beauty of her varied face.'" He continues, Christianity is not "monocultural and monotonous" and unity does not mean cultural uniformity. Instead, he says, "the faith cannot be constricted to the limits of understanding and expression of any one culture."

For many of us, our experiences of understanding God and his Church have been through a European-American lens. Just go into any church. How are God and Jesus depicted? How about the angels, Mary, and other saints? Go to a Catholic conference. What do the speakers look like? What values do they hold? When we only view our faith from our tiny, subjective, European-American viewpoint, we're desperately missing out. The Lord in his divinity

65

and the Catholic Church in its universality breaks and transcends borders.

On one hand, embracing diversity means expanding my love and understanding of a universal Church on a conceptual level. On the other hand, embracing diversity means embracing the person who is different from me. So how do I practically do that? It's not by eliminating diversity and putting a monocultural blanket over differences. It's not by displaying some cheesy stock photo of people of different races holding hands.

Instead, embracing diversity means widening my heart and social circle to fit people who do not look like me. It means allowing myself the time to really look at others, to be in awe of their dignity, and to mentally genuflect at their sacredness. It means to see someone wholly, as body and soul, by not (1) ignoring race or (2) reducing someone's identity to his or her race by using jokes or stereotypes. Instead, embracing diversity means seeing every person as complex. Embracing diversity is saying, "You belong in the Church, I belong in the Church, and with you and me, the Church looks more like heaven."

## COOL SAINT
# MARIAN APPARITIONS

In apparitions across centuries and countries, our Blessed Mother has appeared to us in different ethnicities, often dressed in traditional local garments. Our Lady of Guadalupe is one example of this. If you don't know it already, research the story and all the mind-blowing facts of this miraculous image.

But I want to focus on how we can tell from the image that Mary, in her humility and maternal intuition, intentionally chose to come close to the natives of Mexico. The mantle of our Lady is turquoise, which was the color of the gods and of royalty. The dress that she is wearing is covered in Aztec flowers, a symbol of an Aztec princess. On her womb is a four-petal flower, which is an Aztec symbol of life and deity. Additionally, the angel supporting her would have indicated to the Mesoamericans that she is royalty, as only kings and queens would be carried on someone's shoulders. All of these symbols were there for the native people to know God in a way they would relate to and understand. Today, people in Mexico call her *La Virgen Morena* or "the Brown Virgin." Her skin color matters to them. If Mary is our model of faith and she embraces the diversity of the Church in this way, then so should we.

## FORGOTTEN PRAYER
## THE UNIVERSAL PRAYER

We're not likely to forget the Our Father, but we probably forgot that other people say the Our Father too. Search the Our Father in a different language. Allow yourself to wonder who has said these sacred words before, what their stories are, why they pray this prayer, and whether certain words have slightly different connotations than how you understand them. Listen to a recording of the Our Father in a different language. Are the words spoken in a monotone, or does it sound like they're being sung?

## LIVING THE FAITH

Expose yourself to the wider church. Go to a Mass celebrated in a different language or attend a special cultural event held by the parish. Learn about a saint who is not from Europe or a saint whom a culture has a strong devotion to. Read books that reflect Catholic and Christian experiences in other parts of the world.

# BRINGING CATHOLIC TWITTER INTO THE REAL WORLD

## Tommy Tighe

In the original *Catholic Hipster Handbook*, I referred to Twitter as "either one of the greatest things on earth or one of the worst" and "both a tool that brings us together and a wedge that splits us apart." It feels somewhat odd to say that the Catholic corners of Twitter have played such a huge role in my faith life. Not only because it directly led to the first book deal (not kidding) but also because of the relationships I've formed with others, 280 characters at a time.

It can be easy to overlook the deep friendships and spiritual bonding happening on Twitter. After all, a quick glance at the timeline seems to provide little more than ironic jokes and weird memes that don't make sense unless you're *always* logged on. Scratching the surface a bit, however, shows us there is something deeper happening. Amid all the weird humor is a welcoming group of committed Catholics who care about one another, work hard to push one another further in the spiritual life, and actually pray for one another *in the moment* rather than just smashing the like button when prayers are requested. In fact, I have come to see Catholic Twitter as the archetype for what all of our local parish communities *should* be.

I'm serious.

Twitter has been incredible for Catholics. We use it to evangelize, to share the Good News of the Gospel, and to realize that there are a ton of people out there *just like us.* A lot of people on Catholic social media say, "I wish we all lived close to each other! It would be so cool!" But here's the deal: We *do* live within a community of Catholics who share our faith, our values, and sometimes even our sense of humor. We just have to step away from our screens and be willing to make ourselves available to those around us.

It isn't a stretch to say that someone you know on Catholic Twitter might be sitting a few pews away from you at Mass on Sunday, and you don't even know it! That sense of community we have all found online, that beautiful sense of belonging and caring for one another, needs to be brought into the real world. If we can pull that off, we will undoubtedly revitalize our parishes and once again move them toward being beacons of light to the world around us.

Just to serve up one example of what I mean here: Catholics on Twitter have been known to send care packages to their "mutuals" when they're going through a difficult time, in need of a pick-me-up, or just because. Imagine that: two people who only know each other through retweets, likes, and GIFs have grown in relationship close enough to actually send each other packages filled with love, support, and encouragement! I have come home from work surprised to see an unexpected box sitting on the porch, only to open it up and find holy cards, relics, cool t-shirts, and *even all the fixings to make homemade poutine* (shout out to my Canadian Catholic sisters and brothers).

It's beautiful.

But we have to remember that there are tons of families, single folks, and even priests and religious in our own communities who could use the same show of love and support. We need to take what we've learned and developed from the Catholic Twitterverse and bring it into our communities. If we develop solid relationships with those around us, in our communities and in our parishes, it'll be worth more than all retweets in the world.

## COOL SAINT
## VENERABLE PATRICK PEYTON, C.S.C.

Born in 1909 in County Mayo, Ireland, the "Rosary Priest" came to the United States in 1927 and turned his life around from being a rebellious teenager to one of the most effective evangelizers of the Catholic faith in modern American history. His pithy quips such as "The family that prays together stays together" and "A world at prayer is a world at peace" would have fit quite perfectly in today's world of tweets and short social media posts. He was also unafraid to think big, putting on large rallies for the Rosary right smack-dab in the middle of secular culture, including famous gatherings in San Francisco (where 500,000 people gathered to pray the Rosary together) and Rio de Janeiro (where 1.5 million gathered together).

*Venerable Patrick Peyton*, pray for us.

## FORGOTTEN PRAYER
## PRAYER FOR A FAVOR THROUGH VENERABLE PATRICK PEYTON

God, our Father,
your wisdom is displayed in all creation
and the power of your grace is revealed
in the lives of holy people
who inspire us to trust you more fully
and to serve others more generously.
In a unique way,
you blessed the life and work of your servant
Fr. Patrick Peyton, C.S.C.,
and made him a fervent apostle of Mary,
Queen of the Holy Rosary and Mother of us all.
Through his intercession,
we ask for this favor . . .
Please grant it, if it is for your honor and glory,
through Christ Our Lord.
Amen.

## LIVING THE FAITH

Last time around we gave you a list of some quality Catholic Twitter accounts to follow, but this time we're encouraging you to develop relationships similar to the ones you've developed on Twitter—but in real life.

So, after Mass this Sunday, introduce yourself to someone outside of church. I know. I'm an introvert too. I'm terribly anxious just thinking about walking up to someone and saying hi after Mass. *But we have to do it.* We have to develop relationships in our communities in order to strengthen the Body of Christ in our communities as well as ourselves.

And who knows, you might even end up running into someone who has the same taste in memes.

# PUNK ROCK CATHOLICISM [AKA TATTOOS]

Theresa Zoe Williams

I was raised in a conservative, middle-class, white, Catholic family in rural Pennsylvania. I was raised to be clean-cut and look "respectable"—one ear piercing in each lobe, natural-colored hair long enough to be pulled into a ponytail, and ink-free skin. But here I am with two lobe piercings in each ear, purple hair, and tattoos—a far cry from the outward appearance I was raised to give off!

Growing up, the only people who seemed to have tattoos were gang members, bikers, and sailors; basically, people who were considered "rough around the edges" and with whom you shouldn't associate. In the 1990s and 2000s, punk culture started to become a bigger staple in the mainstream music and television scenes and so did the popularity of crazy hair colors, alternative piercings, and tattoos. Some people used getting tattoos as a way to belong to that crowd or to set themselves apart from what was acceptable in the mainstream.

Nowadays, more people have alternative piercings—think nose or cartilage—neon-colored hair, and tattoos, and a load of them go to Mass every Sunday! I think the rise in popularity of tattoos among Catholics is mainly due to two factors:

1. People are tired of conforming to arbitrary standards that have little to no moral bearing.
2. People want visible reminders of their beliefs, joys, and triumphs and to tell more of their personal stories and histories visibly.

"Preach the Gospel at all times, and if necessary, use words." This bit of wisdom is usually attributed to St. Francis of Assisi, and though its authorship is debated, its point remains: our words should be secondary, an affirmation of our deeds and how we live our lives. Normally, you can't tell just by looking at someone what values, ideals, or beliefs he or she holds, so you look for external or visible clues, such as how the person treats others. But if a guy has a cross tattoo, you'd probably rightly assume that he's Christian. If a woman has an image of the Blessed Virgin Mary on her upper arm, you'd probably rightly assume that she's Catholic. Tattoos can offer a physical and visual invitation to speak with and learn about one another. People with tattoos are often asked questions such as, "What does that mean?" or "Why'd you get that?" What a perfect opportunity for conversation and evangelization!

My two current tattoos (I may have more by the time you read this) are neither overtly Catholic nor in English, so people often ask me what they say. I then have the privilege of telling the questioners about their significance. They say "grace" and "mercy" in Gaelic and Polish, respectively, to remind me of God's gifts to us. They are on my wrists to help me constantly call to mind Christ's sacrifice on the Cross and to remind me of my role and calling as a writer. I chose the Gaelic and Polish languages to honor my mother, who was Irish and Polish. I chose "mercy" specifically to be in Polish because the image of and devotion to Divine Mercy was given to us in Poland and also because John Paul II was known as "the pope of mercy" and was also Polish. So through two simple words on my body, I am able to proclaim the Good News, share a significant part of my story, remind myself of my beliefs and devotions, and connect with another soul.

Neither the Catholic Church nor God prohibit tattoos. Ancient Christians understood all of this. Traditionally, pilgrims to the Holy Land and Crusaders would get tattoos of Jerusalem crosses and the like to commemorate their visits and to give glory to God through their bodies by having permanent, visible reminders of their faith for themselves and everyone they encountered. If used in this way, tattoos can be a beautiful tribute to God and a sign of grace to those we encounter. When St. Thomas finally saw the Resurrected Christ, the first thing Christ asked him to do was to touch his wounds—those outward symbols that did not go away after the Resurrection but that remained as a reminder of this new life given to us. Just as Christ allowed an outward sign of the miraculous gift of salvation to remain on his body though it was unnecessary, so too can tattoos function as such for us today.

## COOL SAINT
## ST. VERONICA GIULIANI

St. Veronica Giuliani was born on December 27, 1660, in Mercatello, Italy, the last of seven sisters. She was given the name Orsola at Baptism and displayed spiritual sensitivity and devotion from a very young age.

When she was seventeen, she entered the strict cloister of the monastery of Capuchin Poor Clares, after convincing her father to allow her to do so instead of marrying. She was given the name Veronica, which means "true image," and she did, in fact, become a true image of the Crucified Christ. While in the cloister, St. Veronica configured herself ever more closely to Christ through penance, suffering, and mystical experiences.

When St. Veronica was thirty-four, she received the marks of the crown of thorns on her forehead; at thirty-seven, she received the stigmata. She asked Jesus to allow her to be crucified with him. She wrote of the experience, saying, "In an instant, I saw five radiant rays issue from His most holy wounds; and they all shone on my face. And I saw these rays become, as it were, little tongues of fire. In four of them were the nails; and in one was the spear, as of gold, red hot and white hot: and it went straight through my heart, from one side to the other . . . and the nails pierced my hands and feet. I felt great pain but in this same pain I saw myself, I felt myself totally transformed into God."[1]

The stigmata gave her much tribulation, as her bishop rigorously tested her about her experiences. He removed her from ordinary community life for a time and allowed her to go to Mass only on Sunday or holy days. Not once did she become bitter, instead remaining steadfast and obedient. She allowed herself to be not only physically crucified with Christ but also emotionally, psychologically, and spiritually crucified.

Eventually, St. Veronica Giuliani was restored as novice mistress and then, at fifty-six, was elected abbess despite her protests. She died eleven years later at the age of sixty-seven. Her feast day is July 9, and she lies incorrupt in the Capuchin Poor Clare Monastery of Città di Caastello, Italy.

## FORGOTTEN PRAYER
## LITANY OF ST. VERONICA GIULIANI

Kyrie, eleison. Christe, eleison. Kyrie, eleison.

Christ, hear us.
Christ, graciously hear us.

God, the Father of heaven, have mercy on us.
God, the Son, the Redeemer of the world, have mercy
   on us.
God, the Holy Spirit, have mercy on us.
Holy Trinity, one God, have mercy on us.

Holy Mary, Immaculate Conception, pray for us.
Holy Mary, Patroness of the Franciscan order, pray
   for us.
St. Francis of Assisi, Seraphic Father, pray for us.
St. Veronica Giuliani, pray for us.

St. Veronica Giuliani, true image of Jesus Crucified, pray for us.

St. Veronica Giuliani, marked with the wounds of Jesus, pray for us.

St. Veronica Giuliani, Mary's favorite daughter, pray for us.

St. Veronica Giuliani, comforter of the Sacred Heart, pray for us.

St. Veronica Giuliani, pledge of wondrous loyalty, pray for us.

St. Veronica Giuliani, abyss of humility, pray for us.

St. Veronica Giuliani, daughter of holy obedience, pray for us.

St. Veronica Giuliani, model of monastic perfection, pray for us.

St. Veronica Giuliani, mirror of God's beauty, pray for us.

St. Veronica Giuliani, furnace of Divine Love, pray for us.

St. Veronica Giuliani, fire of apostolic zeal, pray for us.

St. Veronica Giuliani, adorned with supernatural graces, pray for us.

St. Veronica Giuliani, bright in holy simplicity, pray for us.

St. Veronica Giuliani, soul consumed by love, pray for us.

## LIVING THE FAITH

It is significant that St. John opens his gospel with a discourse on Christ as the Word. Most significantly, he says, "And the Word became flesh and lived among us" (Jn 1:14). Christ makes our flesh significant. St. Paul echoes the importance of Christ's body and sacrifice and the importance of uniting our bodies to Christ when he writes in Galatians 6:17, "From now on, let no one make trouble for me; for I carry the marks of Jesus branded on my body." Something cool here is that the word "marks" is translated from the word "stigmata" and "stigmata" was also the word used to described branding slaves or making marks on one's body to signify devotion to pagan gods. Essentially, St. Paul is telling us that being joined to Christ in our flesh—through scars from apostolic works, receiving the actual stigmata, or tattoos representing Catholic truths—is good and praiseworthy.

So here's your challenge to live it out: Even if you would never get a tattoo, give it some consideration! Reflect on an aspect of the faith that has a central place in your life, perhaps a certain saint or an image of Mary or a particular cross. Then think about how you would incorporate it into an image on your body and where you would place it. For example, maybe a tattoo on your wrist would help you recall Christ's wounds or a tattoo on your foot would signify journeying. Or maybe you would want one on your forearm, just so you can see it easily and often. Once you've decided all that, use a Sharpie or washable marker to draw it on yourself. Leave it for a week and see the reactions you get to it and how you feel about it. Take the time to pray with your image too. You can even mix it up and try out different images every couple of days. Have fun! But recognize the spiritual intention and attention you give it. Maybe you'll even decide to make it permanent!

# BECOMING INKLINGS

## Kaitlyn Facista

Tucked in the heart of Oxford, there is a cozy old pub called The Eagle and Child. It's the sort of place you might pass by if you didn't know its story, an unassuming old building at the end of a row. And yet others, mostly bookish nerds such as I, have made visits to Oxford specifically for an afternoon spent in this quaint little pub. The Eagle and Child, or "The Bird and Baby" as it's lovingly called, holds a special place in my heart because it was once the meeting place of the Inklings, a literary group in which J. R. R. Tolkien and C. S. Lewis were prominent members. And on this cold and dreary January day, my little family and I found ourselves sharing lunch within its walls.

Just two days earlier, my husband, our daughter, and I had been confirmed into the Catholic Church, and now we were making our very first pilgrimage as Catholics. I can attribute much of my reversion to Christianity to C. S. Lewis and my ultimate conversion to Catholicism to J. R. R. Tolkien, so this trip to Oxford felt a lot like going back to my roots.

The Inklings were an informal literary group that met in the Oxford area in the 1930s and '40s. While members came and went throughout the years, its most consistent, and most notably famous, members included J. R. R. Tolkien, C. S. Lewis, Owen Barfield, and Charles Williams. They could often be found on Tuesday

79

afternoons in this small pub reading aloud and critiquing one another's writing. While they did not follow any formal rules or bylaws, they met regularly for a common purpose, sharing their love for literature and encouraging one another in their work.

As my husband and I shared a pint over lunch, I couldn't help but feel a sense of closeness to the community of authors who sat in this very same corner so many years ago. The memory of their fellowship is the sort of thing that lingers in a place, instilling a sense of purpose and belonging within the hearts of all who enter. And the legacy of the written works they left behind is nothing short of inspiring.

While the Inklings were not a Catholic group (although most of its members were Christians of one form or another), their style of accompaniment toward a common purpose is something we as Catholics should strive to adopt. All too often we find ourselves drifting through life, filling our days with superficial small talk and busywork. But what would happen if, instead, we stepped back, reevaluated our life's goals, and began to intentionally pursue them? What if we could cultivate a community of people who were doing the same? We would change the world.

We all know how much the Catholic Church loves organized groups. There is no shortage of religious orders, lay ministries, and hierarchical clubs for Catholics to choose from. And while these sorts of organizations play an important role within the life of the Church, we often forget that informal community is also important. While we Catholics have a great love for filling out paperwork and following programs, it's good for the soul to regularly set these formalities aside and simply come together for fellowship and conversation.

When we do this, we need to recognize the need for creating a balance between being intentional while remaining laid-back. The Inklings, I think, can serve as a model for us in this way. Within their community we see a group of people who have come together to pursue a common purpose—in their case writing and criticizing literature—but who have done so in a very human way. Their meetings didn't follow any rigid formats, their members came and went throughout the years, and the tone of their meetings varied from academic to lighthearted.

The Inklings spent their time connecting with one another, building trusting relationships, constructively criticizing one another, and journeying toward their collective goal. When rooted in Christianity, this kind of fellowship and authentic community can become a powerful witness to the joy of the Gospel, especially to those who may have been hesitant to attend a formal event hosted at a parish hall. While evangelization for its own sake can often be done poorly and end up being off-putting, evangelization that flows naturally from a thriving community can be incredibly fruitful.

When my husband and I became Catholic, we left behind a vibrant Protestant community for the sake of our conversion, and the lack of anything similar within the Catholic Church felt painfully obvious. The first year following our conversion was one of the loneliest I've ever experienced, and it took a move across the country to finally find a community we could call home. By then, our daughter had grown into a squirmy toddler, and I found myself carrying her into the church narthex during Sunday Mass on the regular. It took a few weeks to begin to recognize other moms in the back of the church, and finally, after a few more weeks, I worked up the courage to say hello to one of them after Mass. She told me she was hoping to start a parish moms' group and invited me to their first playdate soon after. From there, my husband found a community with some of the other dads. And before we knew it, we had an amazing group of friends.

A year later when my husband's new job meant another cross-country move, integrating my family into our new parish was much easier because I knew what to do this time. I got involved in the groups that my parish already had to offer, and I helped start the ones they didn't. After meeting with some of the other mothers, I helped put together a moms' group and we met every other week to pray the Chaplet of Divine Mercy together. We also started attending young adult events, where we made a couple of friends and decided to form a small group of our own. I've learned that sometimes the kind of group you want doesn't exist yet, and it's up to you to make it. You never know when the community you're forming will be an answer to someone else's prayer or what kind of impact your group will have on the world.

As we said goodbye to The Eagle and Child that day, we left filled with a renewed sense of the importance of community, and it's been something we've carried with us for the years ahead. J. R. R. Tolkien's The Lord of the Rings and C. S. Lewis's The Chronicles of Narnia are two of the world's best-selling book series, and I can't help but see a connection between their literary fellowship and their literary success. We were made for fellowship, and the legacy of their friendship serves as a bright reminder that in supporting one another, we can accomplish great things.

## COOL SAINT
## ST. FRIDESWIDE

Because of the Inklings' tie to Oxford, I want to introduce you to the city's patron saint. St. Frideswide, patroness of Oxford, was a Benedictine hermitess and nun who lived from about 665 to 735. She was the daughter of pious royalty and formed a small community of religious sisters in Oxford at a young age. Although she had committed herself to a vow of celibacy, she was pursued by a prince who had determined to abduct and marry her. Upon learning of his plans, she fled to the forest and found refuge in an abandoned hut. There, a fountain miraculously sprang up at her prayer, and she was able to survive in hiding for about three years.

She eventually returned home to Oxford, and the enraged prince besieged the city. Frideswide desperately called upon saints Catherine and Cecilia for protection, and at their intercession, the prince was struck blind the moment he stepped foot into Oxford. At this, the siege was ended and Frideswide returned to her convent, where her community grew and thrived for many years. According to some, the University of Oxford has its origin in the school founded there. Upon her death on October 19, 735, Frideswide was buried in her monastery, where the Church of England's Christ Church Cathedral now stands. Her feast day is October 19.

St. Frideswide, pray for us!

## FORGOTTEN PRAYER
# DEDICATION OF A FAMILY OR COMMUNITY

Jesus, our brother and our Lord, you have come to save us because God loves us with a deep and unending love. You have given us Mary, your mother, to be our mother too, and invite us to follow her example. On earth she was a woman of faith and prayer, of obedience to God's will, always ready to serve in any way. In heaven she continues to pray for us, so that we may serve God faithfully in our daily living.

Jesus, help us to ponder in our hearts the many ways you show your love in our lives, and lead us to walk with your mother as we follow you each day.

Jesus, we praise you, for you are our Lord and our God for ever and ever.

Amen!

## LIVING THE FAITH

What are you passionate about? Do you know anyone else who has similar interests? Spend a minute reflecting on a few of your life's passions or goals, and then find a few people who are pursuing something similar. It doesn't have to be specifically Catholic. It could be a physical activity such as running or another shared hobby, interest, or goal. Ask a couple of friends if they'd like to join. Pick a day, perhaps once or twice a month to begin with, and plan to meet regularly at this time. I know life gets busy, but being consistent with your time commitment helps create stability within your group. Next, decide on a name. All good groups have a cool name. Then think of a meeting place, and there you go. You have a club. Boom. Done. Keep in mind the sort of community formed within the Inklings for your group, striving for intentional yet informal community.

# HUMAN FORMATION FOR EVERY CATHOLIC

Fr. Damian Ference

On March 25, 1992, Pope John Paul II published *Pastores Dabo Vobis*. The English translation is *I Will Give You Shepherds*, and the document deals with the formation of seminarians and the ongoing formation of priests. Note that the document was published on the Feast of the Annunciation, which celebrates the moment that God took on flesh in the womb of Mary. Next to Christmas, it is the most incarnational day of the liturgical year.

I am convinced that John Paul II chose to publish *Pastores Dabo Vobis* on the Feast of the Annunciation because of the groundbreaking incarnational contribution he would make to priestly formation that year. Before 1992, there were three basic domains of priestly formation: spiritual, intellectual, and pastoral. That made sense. We want our priests to be spiritual, we need them to know the faith, and we hope that they will be able to take care of the faithful through their pastoral ministry. But John Paul II noticed that there was something missing, something very important.

Human beings are spiritual beings, but we are not only spiritual; we are also human. Therefore, as human beings, we can never be spiritual apart from being human. Remember that when God the Father sent his only Son to save us from sin in the person of Jesus

Christ, Jesus came to us as one of us in all things but sin. The Second Person of the Trinity came to us as one of us, while remaining God—that's the mystery of the Incarnation. Athanasius puts it this way: "God became man so that man could become God."[1] So how do we become God? How do we become holy? We can only become holy through our humanity and never apart from it.

In *Pastores Dabo Vobis*, John Paul II insists that the first domain of priestly formation is not the spiritual but the human. He calls human formation "the necessary foundation" of all formation. This isn't to say that spiritual formation isn't important—after all, John Paul II calls it "the heart for formation"—but it is to say that we have no access to our spirituality apart from our humanity. Even the most spiritual things we do are always done as human beings. We can't escape being human, nor should we want to. It's what we are. It's how we have access to God and all of his creation.

So what does human formation mean in the life of a seminarian or a priest? It means that priests cannot ignore the human issues. It means addressing one's family history, understanding of self, friendships, sexual history, financial habits, as well as one's general and specific joys and disappointments in life. It also means paying attention to things such as nutrition, exercise, sleeping patterns, hygiene, and time management. Think about it. Those are all important in the life of a seminarian and a priest.

One of the greatest compliments that I think a priest can receive is to be told that he is very human. Most of the time, when someone recognizes that a priest is human, that person is recognizing holiness, because when a priest is holy, his humanity becomes very attractive. In *Pastores Dabo Vobis*, John Paul II wrote, "It is important that the priest should mold his human personality in such a way that it become a bridge and not an obstacle to others in their meeting with Jesus Christ the Redeemer of humanity" (43). Think about the best priests that you know personally. Why are they great? Because they have allowed the Lord to live within their very flesh, their very humanity, and you have encountered

Christ in them. They are not simply very spiritual priests; they are also very human.

In Christianity it is impossible to be holy apart from one's humanity. And this is true not only for priests but also for all the faithful. This is why, if you are looking to grow in holiness, the place to start is by looking at your humanness and by looking to the One who took on our humanity in order to give us access to his divinity. Too often people try to escape into some gnostic spiritual realm to find their salvation, which is anti-Christian precisely because it's anti-incarnational. We can never find our salvation apart from our humanity because God came to save us not as an angel but as a human being, while remaining God.

So where might you begin your human formation? Ask yourself these three questions:

1. What do I think about most?
2. What passions, emotions, and feelings are most common to me during the day or when I'm falling asleep at night?
3. What do I desire?

Don't make the mistake of rushing to answer these questions and thinking you already have the answer. Take your time. Most of us aren't reflective enough to know our true thoughts, emotions, and desires immediately. After a prayer to the Holy Spirit for guidance, try journaling or talking to a good friend who is an attentive listener. Soon you will find the answers to these questions. Then bring those answers—your humanity—to Jesus. Only when you are honest with all that you are can you give all that you are to the One who gives us all of himself.

Jesus entered into our humanity to bring us his divinity. But the only way we have any access to his divinity is through our humanity. So let's stop trying to live as angels and start living the life of holiness as human beings.

## COOL SAINT
## ST. JOHN PAUL II

John Paul II is the go-to saint for assistance in human formation. I remember being a senior in high school in 1994 and seeing pictures of JPII as young Fr. Wojtyla, accompanying his young people in the mountains of Poland both in a kayak and on a pair of skis. He also wore Chuck Taylors with his cassock back in the 1950s, which is pretty rad.

St. John Paul II had a great devotion to the Incarnation, and it's on display in all his writings, most especially his Theology of the Body. He can help you discover your deepest thoughts, feelings, and desires and show you how to share them with the Lord, especially in the areas of family history, relationships, and human sexuality, which can often be some of the trickiest areas to navigate in life.

## FORGOTTEN PRAYER
## PRAYER OF PREPARATION FOR THE CHALICE AT HOLY MASS (ROMAN MISSAL)

> By the mystery of this water and wine may we come to share in the divinity of Christ who humbled himself to share in our humanity.

## LIVING THE FAITH

Make a list of the ten things that are most important to you. Then make a holy hour and reflect on how God desires to be present to you and with you in all those things. Remember, if something is important to you, it's also very important to God; and figuring out how your loves are connected to God's love for you is at the heart of human formation.

# I'VE GOT THAT GRIEF, GRIEF, GRIEF, GRIEF DOWN IN MY HEART

## Tommy Tighe

> Life is pain, highness. Anyone who says differently is
> selling something.
> —Dread Pirate Roberts, *The Princess Bride*

*The Princess Bride* may be little more than a fun and lighthearted comedy, one of the best ever in my humble opinion, but this line delivered by Westley (still in the role of the Dread Pirate Roberts at the time) has a piercing truth I like to avoid thinking about as often as possible.

The Bible has quite a bit to say about this idea as well: "I am now rejoicing in my sufferings for your sake, and in my flesh I am completing what is lacking in Christ's afflictions for the sake of his body, that is, the church" (Col 1:24). "In the world you face persecution. But take courage; I have conquered the world!" (Jn 16:33). "Many are the afflictions of the righteous; but the Lord rescues them from them all" (Ps 34:19).

I could go on and on and on, but the point here is pretty clear: our lives will be filled with suffering.

As I began my reversion back to the Catholic faith in my twenties, I was eager to share my renewed love of the faith with anyone

89

willing to talk to me. I even went online in search of tried-and-true methods of sharing the faith, the top evidence-based approach to evangelization. And, time and time again, my search ended with one recommendation: be joyful. The idea was to allow the love of God to make you joyful *all the time*, thus attracting people with your joy and piquing their interest in the reason for the joy within you.

Be a happy, smiling Catholic, and you'll convince people to want to be Catholic!

It sounded nice, but based on my personal life experience, it didn't resonate as authentic for me. While I would generally consider my life to be pretty blessed in the grand scheme of things, I have battled my fair share of trials and tribulations. From a childhood illness that left my body paralyzed at times to the unexpected death of my mother at a relatively early age to miscarriage to the death of a newborn, there were many times when I didn't feel like life was making it very easy to be that joyful Catholic the internet was telling me to be. Smiling through the pain, telling people that I felt blessed and joyful despite everything falling to pieces around me, just didn't seem authentic (let alone possible, if I'm being truly honest with myself).

But as I have moved through my life, I have come to realize that I (and quite possibly *a whole lot* of those internet resources) was missing the whole point. Being joyful isn't about being happy and smiling no matter your circumstances here on earth. Far from it! "In the world you face persecution. But take courage; I have conquered the world!" Jesus didn't promise us the earthly idea of joy we have all come to expect (and sometimes demand) from him. Instead, in this verse he's reminding us that "life is pain," yet we can still have joy because of *what comes next*. His Passion and Crucifixion appear from the world's eyes to be an absolute failure. Only through eyes of faith can we see the redemption and salvation that came through his suffering. Likewise, as St. Paul mentioned, we can rejoice in our suffering, not because we are called to be joyful no matter what but because we know that Jesus called those who suffer blessed and that there is joy, peace, and happiness waiting for them (and all of us) in the eternal life we are being called to.

This is the kind of joy that attracts people to the Catholic faith: a joy that may not be seen externally, or even felt internally, but a joy that manifests itself by continuing to push on in faith even when it doesn't seem worth it. A joy that leads to us showing up for Mass even when we're angry at God. A joy that gets us to pick up our rosaries and pray even though we feel spiritually dry.

These outward signs in the midst of grief are exactly the kinds of things our world needs to see. If we can figure out how to push forward through grief with this kind of joy, the world might just have a fighting chance.

## COOL SAINT
## ST. GEMMA GALGANI

The first saint who popped in my head when I tried to think of a holy hero who embodied what I'm trying to get at here was St. Gemma Galgani.

Born in 1878, Gemma was the fifth of eight children who experienced the death of multiple members of her family at the hands of tuberculosis at a very young age. At the age of twenty-one, Gemma began to experience the stigmata and reported that she experienced visions and had conversations with her guardian angel, the Blessed Mother, and various other saints (most especially St. Gabriel of Our Lady of Sorrows).

She was denied the opportunity to join the Passionists due to her declining health, and she accepted this suffering with exactly the kind of joy we're talking about here. She died at the age of twenty-five and quickly became one of the most famous saints associated with the Passionist movement.

St. Gemma Galgani, pray for us.

## FORGOTTEN PRAYER
# PRAYER IN TIME OF SUFFERING AND NEED[1]

All make the Sign of the Cross. The leader begins:

God comforts us in all our afflictions.
Blessed be God forever.
R/. Blessed be God forever.

Then the Scripture is read:

Listen to the words of the Book of Job (7:3–7, 11):

So I have been assigned months of misery,
and troubled nights have been told off for me.
If in bed I say, "When shall I arise?"
Then the night drags on;
I am filled with restlessness until the dawn.
My flesh is clothed with worms and scabs;
my skin cracks and festers;
My days are swifter than a weaver's shuttle;
they come to an end without hope.
Remember that my life is like the wind;
I shall not see happiness again.

My own utterance I will not restrain;
I will speak in the anguish of my spirit;
I will complain in the bitterness of my soul.

Reader: The Word of the Lord.
R/. Thanks be to God.

After a time of silence, all join in prayers of intercession
and in the Lord's Prayer. Then the leader prays:

God of all mercies, God of all consolation,
comfort us in our afflictions
that we in turn might comfort those who are in trouble
with the same consolation we have received.

Grant this through Christ our Lord.

R/. Amen

All make the Sign of the Cross as the leader concludes:
Let us bless the Lord.
R/. Thanks be to God.

## LIVING THE FAITH

We all know someone who is suffering, grieving, or going through a difficult journey right now, and we have a way to help them. Loneliness is one of the most difficult parts of suffering—feeling absolutely alone, as if there's no one else on earth who can understand what we're going through. In addition, many of the people we might expect to comfort us in our sorrows are uncomfortable sitting in the suffering, and keep their distance while they wait for us to "get over it."

We need to be the people who are able to sit with our suffering sisters and brothers and not be afraid of staying with them when they're in a dark place. We need to be the people who bring Christ to them, and like Christ, sit with them as long as it takes for them to feel love and supported.

Pick up the phone and be that person for someone today.

# CATHOLIC FEMINISM [AKA THINGS POPES SAID THAT NO ONE TALKS ABOUT]

## Samantha Povlock

In 1995, Pope John Paul II wrote, "It depends on (women) to promote a 'new feminism' which rejects the temptation of imitating models of 'male domination,' in order to acknowledge and affirm the true genius of women in every aspect of the life of society and overcome all discrimination, violence, and exploitation."[1]

Pause. Reread that.

Many Catholics today may be surprised that a pope—much less a pope who's a canonized saint—said women should "promote . . . feminism." And yet, those are his words—not mine. In fact, John Paul II was so committed to getting women involved in all areas of society that he said it should be put into law if needed: "The growing presence of women in social, economic and political life at the local, national and international levels is thus a very positive development. Women have a full right to become actively involved in all areas of public life, and this right must be affirmed and guaranteed, also, where necessary, through appropriate legislation" (1995 World Day of Peace Address).

He wasn't just tossing around a cultural buzzword—the pope meant business. Concern for the equality of men and women is deeply Catholic because it's rooted in our understanding of human dignity and complementarity. Although different, men and women are "created . . . in perfect equality," says the *Catechism* (355).

Conversations about feminism and faith require a lot of nuance because modern feminist solutions to women's issues often contradict Catholic teachings. Yet feminists and Catholics can often find common ground in first identifying the issues women face and the need to respond.

For example, more than fifty years ago, Pope John XXIII applauded the fact that "women are gaining an increasing awareness of their natural dignity. Far from being content with a purely passive role or allowing themselves to be regarded as a kind of instrument, they are demanding both in domestic and in public life the rights and duties which belong to them as human persons."[2] Our common human dignity as men and women created in the image of God endow us with certain rights, including the right to be involved in both domestic and public life. Women working to claim this right is absolutely affirmed in our Catholic tradition. In fact, working for equality between the sexes helps establish peace in the world.

In 2007, Pope Benedict XVI asserted that "inadequate consideration for the condition of women helps to create instability in the fabric of society. . . . There can be no illusion of a secure peace until these forms of discrimination are also overcome, since they injure the personal dignity impressed by the Creator upon every human being."[3]

Upholding the dignity of all people is essential for peace-building. Therefore, with regard to all the ways women are still being discriminated against, actively oppressed, or simply overlooked, Catholics are called to work to overcome them.

## COOL SAINT
# ST. TERESA BENEDICTA OF THE CROSS (AKA EDITH STEIN)

Edith Stein was a renowned philosopher and speaker on women's issues in Europe in the early twentieth century. She was raised Jewish, and after a stint as an atheist, converted to Catholicism as a young adult. While waiting to enter the convent, Edith gave numerous speeches on women's education, spirituality, and role in public life that were later compiled into *Essays on Woman*. It is said that her work influenced John Paul II's Theology of the Body.

Raised by a single mom after the age of two, when her father died, Edith experienced firsthand the resilience and vast capabilities of a woman called to offer much to others. Edith's writings expand the image of femininity beyond traditional stereotypes we often encounter and paint a powerfully insightful vision of complementarity and its role in saving souls and the world.

## FORGOTTEN PRAYER
# PRAYER OF ST. TERESA OF AVILA

Let nothing disturb you,
Let nothing frighten you,
All things pass away:
God never changes.
Patience obtains all things.
He who has God
Finds he lacks nothing;
God alone suffices.

## LIVING THE FAITH

Commit to intentionally recognizing and celebrating the gifts of women around you.

Encourage a woman in your parish to take on a leadership role. Call or text a woman you know and affirm how you see her making an impact in her home or work. The next time there is an open job opportunity, speaker need, or committee member opening, nominate a woman for a seat at the table.

Do some reflection and consider whether you perceive more "feminine" attributes such as vulnerability and sensitivity to be weaknesses. Pray about where you see these qualities in Mary and whether you perceive her as weak.

Put a stop to jokes that imply women are subordinate to or less than men. (You know the ones: "Make me a sandwich," "Don't be such a girl," etc.) Read up and reflect on the diversity of women God chose to work through in our Catholic tradition, women such as Judith, Esther, Mary Magdalene, and Joan of Arc.

# THE EARLY CHURCH *WAS* THE CATHOLIC CHURCH

## Holly Vaughan

Throughout this book, you are learning about some of the long-standing practices and beliefs of the Catholic faith, many of which go back centuries. There is no other church that has as long of a history and tradition as the Catholic Church—simply because no other Christian church has been around as long as we have! Many a convert has set out on a search for the early Church—the Church that Jesus himself founded—and followed the trail of bread crumbs right to the front door of the local Catholic parish. Let's look at a few reasons why, starting with the hierarchy that has been around from the very beginning.

Most Catholics are familiar with apostolic succession. We can trace our popes and bishops in an unbroken line right back to St. Peter, who was appointed by none other than Jesus Christ. The Gospel of Matthew 16:18–19 tells us that Jesus says to Peter, "And I tell you, you are Peter, and on this rock I will build my church, and the gates of Hades will not prevail against it. I will give you the keys of the kingdom of heaven, and whatever you bind on earth will be bound in heaven, and whatever you loose on earth will be loosed in heaven." This is where Peter was appointed the first pope, and every pope since that time has been directly linked to him. This is why we call the pope the successor of Peter. In terms of the way the hierarchy operates, we also see that the first Council of the Church is actually recorded in scripture (Acts 15)—the Council of Jerusalem. If you read this account you will see that the apostles (bishops) all met to discuss the issue at hand (circumcision) and that it is Peter (the pope) who addresses them all and makes clarifications. Here we have a prototype of the way councils are still held in our Church today.

Our Church doctrine can also be traced back to the time of the apostles, and the Catholic Church is the only church that has not changed its teachings with the times. A document exists—called the Didache—that is a collection of teachings from the apostles. You can read the Didache online, and even a cursory reading will show that many issues the Church faces today were clarified by the apostles even back in the first century. You will also see that everything they taught then, the Church still teaches today.

The biggest and most important factor that clearly shows the Church's identity as the early Church is also the source and summit of our faith—the Eucharist—as well as the Mass as a whole. When you read the writings of the early Church Fathers about worship, you cannot help but recognize the same Mass that we participate in today. Consider these words written by St. Justin Martyr, in his *First Apology*.

> And on the day called Sunday, all who live in cities or in the country gather together to one place, and the memoirs of the apostles or the writings of the prophets are read, as long as time permits [Liturgy of the Word]; then, when the reader has ceased, the president verbally instructs, and exhorts to the imitation of these good things [homily]. Then we all rise together and pray ... when our prayer is ended, bread and wine and water are brought, and the president in like manner offers prayers and thanksgivings [Eucharistic Prayer] ... and

> the people assent, saying Amen. . . . And this food is called among us εὐχαριστία [the Eucharist], of which no one is allowed to partake but the man who believes that the things which we teach are true . . . for not as common bread and common drink do we receive these . . . [but as] the flesh and blood of that Jesus who was made flesh.[1]

It simply does not get much clearer than that. This document was written fewer than one hundred years after Jesus walked the earth. The earliest Christians knew that Communion was more than a symbol and that what we consume is quite literally the Body and Blood of Christ, and not in any way bread and wine. There is only one Church that still teaches this exact teaching—and that is the Catholic Church.

This is only the tip of the iceberg on the history of our Church, and the many factors that show that we are, in fact, the Church that Jesus founded, the Church that has been divinely protected for more than 2,000 years (in spite of her very human members and leaders), and the Church that is still guarded and guided by the Holy Spirit today.

## COOL SAINT
## ST. ATHANASIUS

St. Athanasius is a bishop and Doctor of the Church, one of the few saints to carry the title "the Great." and the bearer of some serious nicknames such as "Father of Orthodoxy," "Pillar of the Church," and "Champion of Christ's Divinity." He dedicated most of his life to defending Christ's divinity against the Arian heresy (which denied the divinity of Christ) and was actually exiled at the hands of Arian bishops five different times for his valiant defense. He still kept in touch with his flocks by letter until he was able to return to them. In an effort to get rid of him, the Arians accused him of murdering a Meletian bishop and cutting off his hand. They produced a dried-up human hand as evidence. Athanasius, knowing full well that the bishop was alive and in hiding, informed some of his followers, who located the bishop and brought him to the courtroom covered in a cloth. Athanasius asked the bishops gathered if they would recognize the allegedly murdered bishop if they saw him, and they affirmed that they would. He then pulled the cloth off the bishop, pointed out that he still had both of his hands, and was thereby cleared of all charges. In St. Athanasius we find an example of courage, true orthodoxy, and faithfulness to the true teachings of the church.

## FORGOTTEN PRAYER
## PRAYER TO MARY, THE MOTHER OF GOD, BY ST. ATHANASIUS

It is becoming for you, O Mary, to be mindful of us, as you stand near him who bestowed upon you all graces, for you are the Mother of God and our Queen. Come to our aid for the sake of the King, the Lord God and Master who was born of you. For this reason you are called "full of grace." Be mindful of us, most holy Virgin, and bestow on us gifts from the riches of your graces, O Virgin full of grace. Amen.

## LIVING THE FAITH

Study the history of the Church! Read the Church Fathers' writings, or pick up one of the many books or studies available on the early Church. (Try *The Real Story of Catholic History: Answering Twenty Centuries of Anti-Catholic Myths* by Steve Weidenkopf.) We have to know why we believe what we believe and how to defend our faith against falsities. Knowing our history is a great place to start!

# YOU MUST WAIT THREE DAYS TO SEE THE POPE

## Matthew Sewell

St. Gregory VII was on the list of topics for this book long before we experienced (as the *Catching Foxes* podcast refers to it) the "Summer of Scandal"—the 2018 sex abuse crisis.

It's ironic, really. The eleventh century, in which Gregory VII reigned as pontiff, was a time strikingly similar to our own—civilization as people in the Christian world knew it was crumbling around them. Rome, once a city of more than half a million people, had been reduced to a mere thirty thousand from centuries of barbarian invasions. The clergy of the day largely cast their vows of celibacy to the wind and lived more like princes than as shepherds.

Nepotism at the highest levels let the likes of Benedict IX and others into the papacy. Benedict was the man who was thrice pope: he left once to take a wife, "sold" the papacy to leave the second time, and then was literally chased out of town by soldiers once and for all in 1048.

Thankfully, the tide began to turn with Gregory VII, both when he was serving his immediate predecessors in the papal court and when he was elected to the papacy in 1073 against his own wishes. Gregory was praised by his electors as "a devout man . . . mighty in human and divine knowledge, a distinguished lover of equity and justice, a man firm in adversity and temperate in prosperity."

With the election of Gregory also came what's now known as the *investiture controversy*—an intrusion upon Church affairs by the Holy Roman emperor Henry IV, who sought to choose his own bishops for dioceses residing in his kingdom and also control Church property therein. At first, Henry seemed willing to be the pope's loyal subject, having sent Gregory a gushing letter of apology and submission upon his election. But the deference from the emperor was short-lived.

One of Gregory's first acts of business in 1073 was reforming the clergy by enacting four specific decrees:

1. That clerics who had obtained any grade or office of sacred orders by payment should cease to minister in the Church.
2. That no one who had purchased any church should retain it, and that no one should be permitted to buy or sell ecclesiastical rights.
3. That all who were guilty of incontinence (engaging in any sort of sexual acts) should cease to exercise their sacred ministry.
4. That the people should reject the ministry of clerics who failed to obey these injunctions.[1]

Because of Gregory's strong will and relentless disposition when it came to reforming the broken Church, everyone knew these decrees were anything but a dead letter. And that didn't sit well with many in the Church, particularly in Germany, where it was said that many married clergy would rather renounce their priesthood than conjugal life with their wives, and that "he for whom men were not good enough [referring to the pope] might go seek angels to preside over the Churches."[2]

Henry saw in this dust-up his chance for a power grab, especially since he had just won a crucial battle over the Saxons in 1075, so he began imposing his own choices for bishop, and in the meantime convened a meeting of German bishops (many of whom were no fan of Gregory) and a shady Roman cardinal (also not a fan of Gregory). At the meeting, the bishops renounced their allegiance to the pope, and the emperor boldly declared Gregory deposed.

Gregory, knowing that two could play at that game—not to mention being well-read on the supremacy of the pope—convened a meeting of his own a few months later, in which he not only excommunicated Henry IV but also deposed him as king and sent word to all of his subjects that they were absolved of any allegiance to him, to boot.

Even though Gregory still expressed desire that the throne remain open for Henry, if he would only repent, all of Henry's supporters deserted him almost overnight, threatening to choose a new emperor if he didn't submit to the pope within a year. The pope invited Henry to meet him at Canossa, in northern Italy, in the middle of what happened to be one of the harshest winters on record.

Henry obeyed, and made for Canossa clad only as a penitent, stripped of his royal robes. Gregory, fully remembering how faithless Henry had been on more than one occasion, wasn't about to make it an easy penance for Henry. When the emperor showed up to the castle doors barefoot and in rags, he was refused entry for *three days*, waiting on his knees outside, in a raging blizzard, before the pope agreed to see him.

In what's rightly called one of the most dramatic moments of the Middle Ages, we have for our reflection and veneration a spiritual leader who would literally stop at nothing to do good and eradicate evil in Christ's Church, even when it meant his own eventual ruin. After Henry was restored to power and reinstated into the Church, he ended up double-crossing Gregory one last time, nearly a decade later, for which the pope himself was partially responsible.

In the end, Gregory ended up forced to flee Rome for good after twelve years in the Chair of Peter, stopping first at the Abbey of Monte Cassino and eventually dying in a castle at Salerno in southern Italy. His last words were, "I have loved justice and hated iniquity; therefore I die in exile."

Canonized more than five hundred years after his death, it is easy to think of St. Gregory VII when reading the great line by G. K. Chesterton: "Each generation is converted by the saint who contradicts it most."[3]

Let us pray for the gift and ability to recognize such saints in our time and remember always that the Lord is guiding the Church, perpetually saying to his panicking children amid the turbulent waves, "Why are you afraid? Have you still no faith?"

## COOL SAINT
## ST. GREGORY VII

Hildebrand of Soana, the man who became St. Gregory VII, was born around the year 1020 in Italy and was the son of a carpenter. His uncle was abbot of a monastery in Rome, where Gregory eventually was sent in later childhood for primary education. He stayed into adulthood and lived there as a monk before being called into service as a chaplain for Fr. John Gratian, the man who later briefly reigned as Pope Gregory VI, and whose witness inspired the name choice of Gregory VII. Gregory possessed a towering intellect, and contributed much to the Church beyond just his reforms of the clergy. In fact, St. Paul VI quoted Gregory VII on the Real Presence in his 1965 encyclical *Mysterium Fidei*.

## FORGOTTEN PRAYER
## PRAYER FOR ALL NEEDS (ATTRIBUTED TO ST. CLEMENT I)

We beg you, Lord, to help and defend us.
Deliver the oppressed.
Pity the insignificant.
Raise the fallen.
Show yourself to the needy.
Heal the sick.

Bring back those of your people who have gone astray.
Feed the hungry.
Lift up the weak.
Take off the prisoners' chains.
May every nation come to know that you alone are God,
that Jesus is your Child, that we are your people,
the sheep that you pasture.
Amen.

## LIVING THE FAITH

If the life of St. Gregory has taught us anything, it's that the Lord raises up saints right at the moment when all seems lost. Especially in these times, be intentional in praying not only for our deacons, priests, and bishops (including the Holy Father) but also for your own virtue.

Pray with this quote of Pope Benedict XVI: "Each of us is the result of a thought of God. Each of us is willed. Each of us is loved. Each of us is necessary."[4] In praying with this, consider how the Lord might be asking you to bring more faith, hope, and charity into our world. It's no accident that you're alive at this moment in history. What does the Lord want of you?

# CHALK ON THE DOOR: HOUSE BLESSINGS

Katie Prejean McGrady

There's nothing quite like being home. Why go out, when you can stay home? Why get dressed up, when you can stay in comfy clothes *at home*? Why go spend money at a restaurant or movie theater or socialize *in public*, when you can just stay home? Home is best.

We love our homes—they're places of solace, comfort, respite, and rest. Home is where all our stuff is. It's where we can most be ourselves. It's where we go at the end of a long day. It's where we invite people to come when we want to spend time with them.

Home is, as Elvis famously sang, where the heart is.

It's because our homes are so important and valuable to us and the place where we put down roots, raise our families, gather together, grow together, eat together, and simply "are" together, that they should be a place where the Lord dwells.

I don't just mean that we hang a crucifix on the wall and say, "All right, Jesus is here now," although that is a good thing to do. We are also called to invite the Lord into our homes—to acknowledge his presence in all that we do in our homes, welcoming him to dwell there just as he dwells in our hearts.

A simple way to do this is by having our homes blessed by a priest or deacon on or around the Feast of the Epiphany.

We celebrate the Feast of the Epiphany on January 6, the last day of the Christmas season, marking the visit of the Magi to baby Jesus. The three kings brought gifts to this tiny babe to celebrate his arrival: gold to symbolize his kingship, frankincense to symbolize his divinity, and myrrh to symbolize his death. Ultimately, they gave gifts to the child Jesus, welcoming his arrival into this world—where he "made his home" to dwell among us.

For years, Catholics have had their homes blessed on (or around) the Feast of the Epiphany to welcome the Lord into their homes just as the three kings welcomed the infant Jesus into the world. With holy water, salt, chalk, and a few simple prayers, a priest or deacon is able to bless a home so that it can become a dwelling place for the Lord, under his protection, and a reminder to all who live in the house that it (and they) are marked for Christ.

The opening words of the traditional house blessing capture the spirit of this tradition: "Let us praise God, who fills our hearts and homes with peace."

Would that we all wish this for our homes—places in which we find comfort and peace—that the Lord himself would fill our homes with *his* peace, so that the place we've made our own can also be God's!

As the house blessing is done, a simple prayer is said in every room of the house, challenging all who live there to remember God's presence and be rooted in his power, and to invite Jesus to be a guest in their hearts, minds, souls, and the physical space they occupy each day. After the prayers and blessings are said, the priest or deacon uses the chalk to write above the doorframe a plus sign; the year; the letters C, M, and B, which stand for the names of the three magi—Caspar, Melchior, and Balthazar—and the Latin phrase *Christus mansionemn benedicat*, which translates to "May Christ bless this house."

Catholics like to bless everything—rosaries, water, the medals we wear, even ourselves—and it only makes sense that we would also want to bless our homes on the Feast of the Epiphany, remembering both Jesus' entrance into this world and thus inviting him to enter, and dwell within, our homes.

## COOL SAINT
## ST. JOSEPH

We don't know much about St. Joseph other than he was a carpenter, he was a man of deep faith, and he helped raise Jesus with his wife, Mary. But really, what else do we need to know about this quiet, holy man? That really says it all: that he would humbly and faithfully take Mary *into his home* after she drops the most surprising and shocking news of all—that she's pregnant by the power of the Holy Spirit! He made a home for Mary and a home for Jesus, and thus is an example to all of us of how our homes should always be a place for the Lord.

There are no recorded spoken words of St. Joseph. All we have in scripture are moments of encounter between him and Mary, angels, and Jesus. But in his silence, he says a lot about how we should all make a dwelling place for the Lord in our hearts and in our homes.

## FORGOTTEN PRAYER
## A SIMPLE HOME BLESSING

When Christ took flesh through the Blessed Virgin Mary, he made his home with us, in this world. May he come to dwell in our hearts and in our home, his presence always among us, nurturing our love for one another, comforting us in our sorrows, inspiring us with his teachings, and sharing in our joys. May our home be a place of love, comfort, solace, refuge, and welcome, and may it always reflect the love of the Lord to all who enter here. Amen.

## LIVING THE FAITH

On the Feast of the Epiphany, invite your parish priest over for dinner and a little Epiphany party and ask him to bless your home in the traditional style (get the chalk ready!). Make him some home-made goodies as a thank-you (I've heard priests love brownies), and consider what it means to intentionally invite God into your home.

# SOCIAL JUSTICE IN EVERY SIP

## Tommy Tighe

As I was introduced to the story of Dorothy Day and her incredible devotion to living out the radical call of Jesus to transform our lives, I found myself wanting to be like her in every way possible. I researched her spirituality and found her devotion to the Liturgy of the Hours inspiring. In reference to joining in the universal prayer of the Church, she once famously quipped, "My strength returns to me with my cup of coffee and the reading of the Psalms."[1]

I researched the history of her cofounding the Catholic Worker Movement with the equally inspiring Peter Maurin and felt called to reach out to my local Catholic Worker to see how my family could join in the important work they were doing for the poor in our community. I went so far as to research Dorothy's daily schedule, her favorite type of music, and even her diet, and I found that she was even up for a challenge in what at first glance may seem like unimportant areas.

In December of 1944, Dorothy wrote an article for the *Catholic Worker* newspaper titled "Poverty and Pacifism," where she explored the value of voluntary poverty in the Christian life, which included focusing on the topic of what we choose to eat and drink: "Poverty means non-participation. It means what Peter Maurin calls regional living. This means fasting from tea, coffee, cocoa,

113

grapefruit, pineapple, etc., from things not grown in the region where one lives."[2]

That's right, long before it was cool to be a "locavore" (the term for the presently fashionable concept of solely eating foods produced locally), Peter Maurin and Dorothy Day were advocating this way of life as an opportunity to sacrifice and become more like Our Lord and the Blessed Virgin Mary through embracing a voluntary poverty.

It wasn't just eating locally that concerned Dorothy when it came to making food choices, however. She also pointed out the need to make educated choices about food and drink based on the conditions of the workers bringing these items from the farm to our tables: "One day last winter we bought broccoli which had the label on it of a corporation farm in Arizona or Texas, where we had seen men, women and children working at two o'clock in the morning with miners' lamps on their foreheads, in order to avoid the terrible heat of the day, which often reached 125 degrees. These were homeless migrants, of which there are some million in the United States. For these there is no room at the inn. We ought not to eat food produced under such conditions."[3]

For Dorothy, every action she participated in or avoided had meaning. Every decision, no matter how small it may have seemed, was a decision for or against Our Lord and his teachings.

For all of us, the same opportunities come up each and every day.

Will we choose to educate ourselves, stand up for the conditions of workers and laborers, and unite ourselves with causes that support the dignity of human beings through everything we consume? It's a difficult challenge, to be sure, but it also gives us the opportunity to choose to be faithful in small things.

**COOL SAINT**
## ST. NICHOLAS OF TOLENTINO

This little-known St. Nicholas lived from 1246 to 1305 in Italy and was canonized by Pope Eugene IV back in 1446. St. Nicholas is unofficially known as the patron saint of vegans and vegetarians, as the Augustinian friar took a vow during his life not to eat meat.

It is also said he was tormented by the devil; one time, the devil reportedly beat him with a stick, and that stick was displayed for years in his local church as a sign of his power to overcome darkness and evil. In another episode of demonic attack, St. Nicholas was served a roasted fowl (putting his vow to not eat meat at risk), but after making the Sign of the Cross over the meal, it immediately flew out a window.

Obviously, he had some heavenly power when it came to his food choices.

*St. Nicholas of Tolentino, pray for us.*

**FORGOTTEN PRAYER**
## PRAYERS TO ST. NICHOLAS OF TOLENTINO AND FOR HOLY SOULS IN PURGATORY

O God, source of strength and courage, you gave your beloved preacher, St. Nicholas of Tolentino, the conviction of faith to the very end. Grace us with the ability to translate your teaching into action, remain patient amid hardship, serve the poor and those who suffer, and live as your true and faithful servants.

**LIVING THE FAITH**

Take up the one-month Catholic Farmer's Market Challenge!

Eating locally and supporting local farmers and food producers is a great way to put your money where your mouth is when it comes to supporting Catholic social justice and causes such as subsidiarity. Can you make it an entire month buying all of your fruits and veggies from your local farmer's market rather than tossing your money at a big-name chain supermarket?

If you think you're up to the challenge, make a grocery list and get a move on!

# GETTING INTO THE SPIRIT OF MICHAELMAS

## Haley Stewart

The Feast of the Archangels takes place on September 29.[1] It was formerly referred to as Michaelmas (pronounced Mickel-muss) and called so after St. Michael's Mass (think Christ's Mass becoming Christmas). A holy day of obligation until the eighteenth century, Michaelmas isn't as big a deal as it used to be. But in my humble opinion, we should make Michaelmas a thing again because the archangels (St. Michael, St. Raphael, and St. Gabriel) are worth celebrating!

### ST. MICHAEL

**Name means:** Who is like God?
**Skills:** Led the friends of God in the fight against Lucifer and the fallen angels with the battle cry "Who is like God?" (Answer: no one.)
**Iconography:** St. Michael is often pictured in armor with a sword or spear fighting the devil, who is yelling *non serviam* or "I will not serve" while getting owned by everyone's favorite archangel.

## ST. RAPHAEL

**Name means:** God heals.
**Skills:** Brings healing and protection. St. Raphael heals Tobit's blindness and frees Sarah from a demon in the Book of Tobit.
**Iconography:** St. Raphael is often shown with a staff, representing his care for pilgrims.

## ST. GABRIEL

**Name means:** God is my strength.
**Skills:** Announced the coming of Jesus to Mary and the coming of John the Baptist to Zechariah.
**Iconography:** In images of the Annunciation, he is often shown carrying a lily.

## COOL SAINT
## ST. JOAN OF ARC

St. Joan (Jeanne d'Arc) was a young French peasant girl who was informed by visions of St. Michael the Archangel, St. Catherine of Alexandria, and St. Margaret that she was called to save France from the English during the Hundred Years' War. Guided by her visions, she supported King Charles VII, and her role as a military leader led to his coronation at Reims cathedral. After being captured by the Burgundians and turned over to the British, she was burned at the stake on May 30, 1491. She was declared a martyr in 1456 and canonized in 1920.

## FORGOTTEN PRAYERS
## PRAYER TO ST. MICHAEL

St. Michael the Archangel,
defend us in battle,
be our protection against the wickedness and snares of
  the devil;
may God rebuke him, we humbly pray;

and do thou, O Prince of the heavenly host,
by the power of God, cast into hell
Satan and all the evil spirits
who prowl through the world seeking the ruin of souls.
Amen.

## LIVING THE FAITH

Go to Mass and have friends over for a feast! In the British Isles, Michaelmas was celebrated with an autumnal feast after the fall harvest. A roast goose with apples was traditional fare, but if geese are thin on the ground in your neck of the woods, you could always substitute a turkey or chicken. Add some carrots into the mix because in the Hebrides women would harvest carrots on Michaelmas and make them into bouquets. You'll also want a blackberry cobbler on your table due to a legend about the devil falling into a blackberry bush when he was expelled from heaven by St. Michael. According to this lore, he spit on the blackberries, making them bitter if they're eaten after Michaelmas.

# SERVANT ROYALTY

## Theresa Zoe Williams

Usually, when we hear the words "princess" or "queen" in modern American usage, our thoughts go to people who are spoiled, who accumulate whatever they want, who look down at and snub others, and who situate themselves at the top of social chains, often at the expense of others. Or we think of people who rule over everyone else in a certain way or use their influence to manipulate others into doing what they want. We also might think of those who are out of touch with other people, don't have the common good in mind, and are power hungry. It's not a very nice connotation!

But we know that God is the king of the universe, that Jesus is the Prince of Peace, and Mary is the Queen of Heaven and Earth. And if we are daughters and sons of God, then that makes us princesses and princes in the heavenly order. So how do we reconcile these things?

To be royalty means to have dominion over that which is under your care. God is the king of the universe because he made it all, and then he gave us dominion over the earth to provide for our needs and the needs of one another. Right after creating humankind, God gave dominion of the earth to them: "God blessed them, and God said to them, 'Be fruitful and multiply, and fill the earth and subdue it; and have dominion over the fish of the sea and over the birds of the air and over every living thing that moves upon the earth'" (Gn 1:28). And so, we are to take care of the earth so that it might be able to continue to provide for our needs and the needs of future generations (which we're also commanded to bring forth!). God provided for man by creating and giving all of the things that we would need to live, survive, and thrive on earth, and then he gave us the power to make sure all of these things are used properly. Therefore, to be royalty means to properly use and disperse the goods at our disposal to make sure we and the others around us have what we all need to live well.

A note: Living well does not mean living lavishly. Living well means having the basic necessities needed to survive without fear of poverty, hunger, or illness. Our resources are to be used by all, to procure these necessities for one another. Likewise, though, it does not mean that we cannot have private property or may not have safeguards in place for our own futures, because we can and should! The *Catechism of the Catholic Church* states that "the earth is divided up among men to issue the security of their lives, endangered by poverty and threatened by violence. The appropriation of property is legitimate for guaranteeing the freedom and dignity of persons and for helping each of them to meet his basic needs and the needs of those in his charge. It should allow for a natural solidarity to develop between men" (2402). The *Compendium of the Social Doctrine of the Church* further expounds on this: "The universal destination of gods requires a common effort to obtain for every person and for all peoples the conditions necessary for integral development, so that everyone can contribute to making a more humane world" (175). In exercising our dominion over the created world rightly, we can bond together as a human family, God's family, and take care of each other.

So how does this translate into us being royalty? It means giving what we have at our disposal to those who need it, whether that be to ourselves and our families or others in our communities or the world at large. St. Basil the Great talked about this responsibility often. He said, "The bread which you hold back belongs to the hungry; the coat, which you guard in your locked storage-chest, belongs to the naked; the footwear mouldering in your closet belongs to those without shoes. The silver that you keep hidden in a safe place belongs to the one in need."[1] We must not let fear or greed have a place in our lives, for when we do, we keep for ourselves what we don't need and which thus rightfully belongs to another in need. Neither should we seize control of industry at the expense of others. All of our interactions with the world given to us should be centered around the common good of one another. This is what God did when he created the world and what he charges us to continue to do with it, as his sons and daughters.

A true prince or princess wants the benefit of all the people around him or her. A true prince or princess would make sure that resources were doled out not simply equally but according to need. A true prince or princess would make sure all around them could also exert their rightful dominion over the earth—just like the early community of believers:

> Now the whole group of those who believed were of one heart and soul, and no one claimed private ownership of any possessions, but everything they owned was held in common. With great power the apostles gave their testimony to the resurrection of the Lord Jesus, and great grace was upon them all. There was not a needy person among them, for as many as owned lands or houses sold them and brought the proceeds of what was sold. They laid it at the apostles' feet, and it was distributed to each as any had need. There was a Levite, a native of Cyprus, Joseph, to whom the apostles gave the name Barnabas (which means "son of encouragement"). He sold a field that belonged to him, then brought the money, and laid it at the apostles' feet. (Acts 4:32–37)

## COOL SAINT
# ST. ELIZABETH OF HUNGARY

St. Elizabeth was born to Hungarian king Andrew II and his wife, Gertrude of Merania, on July 7, 1207. Since she was born as royalty, royal responsibilities were pressed on her from a young age. When Elizabeth was a child, her father arranged for her to marry a German nobleman, Ludwig IV of Thuringia, and she was then sent to court of the Landgrave of Thuringia for education at the age of four. Elizabeth's mother was murdered when Elizabeth was only six, and Elizabeth then sought peace through prayer.

Elizabeth and Ludwig were formally married in 1221 when she was fourteen years old, and they had a happy marriage. She bore three children, two of whom became nobility and the third entered religious life. In 1223, Franciscan friars arrived in Thuringia and taught Elizabeth about the ideals of St. Francis of Assisi. Elizabeth decided to live out these ideals and began wearing simple clothes, performed acts of penance, and devoted herself to acts of charity. She took time every day to deliver bread to the hundreds of poor in her land. In 1226, floods and disease struck Thuringia, and Elizabeth devoted herself to caring for the poor, bringing them food and medicine, and even giving away the royals' clothing and goods to the afflicted. She then also had a hospital built and provided for about one thousand poor people daily. And through all of this, she had the support and help of her husband, Ludwig.

One of her most famous miracles is that of the roses. One day, when she was secretly taking bread to the poor, she met her husband and his hunting party on the way. There were rumors at the time that Elizabeth was stealing the riches of the castle. To quell these rumors, Ludwig asked Elizabeth to open her cloak and reveal what she was carrying. When she opened her cloak, white and red roses tumbled out and this proved to Ludwig and the gentry that she was doing the work of God.

On September 11, 1227, Elizabeth's life changed dramatically when Ludwig died from illness. She vowed never to marry again, much to the chagrin of the royal family, and she took vows of celibacy and obedience to her spiritual director. The next year, Elizabeth joined the Third Order of St. Francis and used her dowry to construct a hospital in honor of St. Francis. At that hospital,

Elizabeth and her companions attended to the ill and poor daily, and she continued her other acts of charity and care for the poor.

St. Elizabeth died on November 17, 1231, at the age of twenty-four and was laid to rest in a gold shrine in the Elisabeth Church in Marburg, Hesse. Her feast day is November 17, and she is the patroness of bakers, beggars, brides, charities, death of children, homeless people, hospitals, the Sisters of Mercy, and widows. Perhaps most significantly, Pope emeritus Benedict XVI praised St. Elizabeth as a "model for those in authority."

## FORGOTTEN PRAYER
# LITANY OF ST. ELIZABETH OF HUNGARY

Lord, have mercy on us.
Christ, have mercy on us.
Lord, have mercy on us.

Christ, hear us.
Christ, graciously hear us.

God, the Father of Heaven, have mercy on us.
God, the Son, Redeemer of the world, have mercy on us.
God, the Holy Ghost, have mercy on us.
Holy Trinity, one God, have mercy on us.

Holy Mary, Mother of mercy, pray for us.
Holy Elizabeth, mother of the poor, pray for us.
St. Elizabeth, who didst fear God from thy heart, pray for us.
St. Elizabeth, most fervent in devotion, pray for us.
St. Elizabeth, devout and beloved disciple of Jesus, pray for us.
St. Elizabeth, imitator of blessed Francis, pray for us.
St. Elizabeth, of noblest faith and birth, pray for us.
St. Elizabeth, devoted to all pious offices, pray for us.
St. Elizabeth, whose nights were spent in prayer and contemplation, pray for us.

St. Elizabeth, who wast consoled with heavenly visions,
   pray for us.
St. Elizabeth, beloved of God and man, pray for us.
St. Elizabeth, full of contempt of this world, pray for us.
St. Elizabeth, example of poverty, chastity, and obedi-
   ence, pray for us.
St. Elizabeth, solace of thy husband, pray for us.
St. Elizabeth, mirror of widows, pray for us.
St. Elizabeth, holocaust of penance and humility, pray
   for us.
St. Elizabeth, admirable preacher of meekness, pray
   for us.
St. Elizabeth, despiser of luxuries of the regal house,
   pray for us.
St. Elizabeth, lover of the Cross of Christ, pray for us.
St. Elizabeth, light of all pious women, pray for us.
St. Elizabeth, nourisher of the orphans, pray for us.
St. Elizabeth, always intent on works of mercy, pray
   for us.
St. Elizabeth, consoler of all sorrows, pray for us.
St. Elizabeth, teacher of the poor, pray for us.
St. Elizabeth, seeker of contumely and affronts, pray
   for us.
St. Elizabeth, distributor of thy riches to thy poor neigh-
   bors, pray for us.
St. Elizabeth, patient in adversity, pray for us.
St. Elizabeth, maker of vestments for the poor, pray
   for us.
St. Elizabeth, hospitable receiver of pilgrims and the
   sick, pray for us.
St. Elizabeth, succor of the needy, pray for us.
St. Elizabeth, formidable to demons, pray for us.
St. Elizabeth, example of all spiritual perfection, pray
   for us.
St. Elizabeth, represser of all vain and dissolute conver-
   sation, pray for us.

St. Elizabeth, cheered by angelic choirs in thy last agony,
pray for us.
St. Elizabeth, miraculous in life, pray for us.
St. Elizabeth, helper of our devotions, pray for us.
St. Elizabeth, our sweetest patron, pray for us.

Lamb of God, Who takest away the sins of the world,
spare us, O Lord!
Lamb of God, Who takest away the sins of the world,
graciously hear us, O Lord!
Lamb of God, Who takest away the sins of the world,
have mercy on us, O Lord!
Christ, hear us.
Christ, graciously hear us.

Pray for us, blessed Elizabeth, that we may be made
worthy of the promises of Christ.

Let us pray: Enlighten, O God of compassion, the
hearts of Thy faithful servants, and through the glorious prayers of blessed Elizabeth, make us to despise
the pleasing things of this world, and ever to delight in
the consolations of heaven. Through Christ our Lord.
Amen.

## LIVING THE FAITH

Take a look at your possessions. How many pairs of shoes do you
own? How many blankets? How many comforts? What do you
have in excess in your life? Do you hold back your money from the
homeless beggars on the street for fear that they may not use that
money to your liking? Do you purchase everything new or do you
try to buy things used to keep down waste? Do you keep your heat
up high in the cold months and your air conditioner on cold in
the hot months? Are you being selfish by keeping all of these good
things for yourself and not also helping to provide these goods for
those in need?

Give away your extra shoes and clothes. Provide your extra blankets to homeless shelters. Keep gift cards to restaurants on hand to give to the needy on the streets. Buy what you can from consignment stores or places such as Goodwill. Keep your heat just a little lower or your air conditioning a little warmer than you normally would not only to conserve energy but also to put yourself in solidarity with those who do not have these comforts. Try to buy food that is ethically grown and provides good wages and living and working conditions for their workers. Make a conscious effort to live simply and to help take care of those around you. Our Lady said to St. Bernadette in Lourdes, "I cannot promise you happiness in this life; only in the next." Be a good steward of your goods and the goods at your disposal and do not store up treasures on earth. Take only what you need and give the rest to others who do not have and take solace in the promise of heaven.

# Part 3
# LIVING WITH LOVE

## Tommy Tighe

St. John of the Cross once said, "In the evening of life we will be judged on love alone."[1] This powerful truth is equal parts terrifying and inspiring. Terrifying because upon reflection, most of us realize that we aren't loving others as we are called to. Inspiring because it shows us what Jesus expects of us in the most succinct way possible. He expects us to love.

But how?

Well, believe it or not, Jesus gives us a seemingly never-ending supply of opportunities to love others and to love him through others. We find these opportunities in the tasks of parenting, in accompanying others through their trials, in standing up for those who have been pushed aside, in making an effort to put the needs of others ahead of our own, and even in making the sacrifice to give ourselves as a total gift to another person.

We're going to be judged on how well we responded to the call to love, and this section is all about giving you a game plan for answering the call in a culture that just doesn't seem to get it.

# HIPSTER MOM: WORKING CATHOLIC MOM OF NINE

Jackie Francois Angel

She raised saints. She is a saint. And her husband is a saint. Catholic family #squadgoals? Check. And before side hustles were a thing, she even had her own small business as a lace maker—in the 1800s. Totally fierce working mama? Check. Her daughter St. Thérèse of Lisieux may be the Catholic version of Instagram-famous (her statue is in almost every church I've ever been in), but St. Zélie Martin would be so overjoyed that souls are still being brought to Jesus through her family a hundred-plus years later. For that was her (and her husband's) goal: to raise a family for God.

With five daughters becoming nuns, one of them officially canonized (St. Thérèse) and another in the process of canonization (Venerable Léonie Martin), they accomplished that goal. But lest you're tempted to think that this family lived in some sort of Catholic candy-land-fairy-tale-dream-world, think again. While Zélie and Louis had a beautiful marriage (she once said about him in a letter, "My husband is a holy man, and I wish that all women could have such husbands")[1] *and* they had nine children together *and* they had successful businesses (Louis as a watchmaker and Zélie as a lace maker), they experienced a great deal of life's suffering. Zélie was stricken with breast cancer, which she endured for ten

131

years until her death at the age of forty-six. Even then through all the pain, Zélie resigned herself to God's will and even still had a good sense of humor. While everybody around her was pleading for a miracle for her healing, Zélie joked, "If I were the Blessed Virgin, I would yield very quickly to so many prayers just to get rid of all these people."[2]

Zélie and Louis also endured the deaths of four of their nine children (two newborn boys, a five-year-old daughter, and a six-week-old girl), who all died within a span of three years. Some people told Zélie that it would have been better for her not to have had those children. As you can imagine, Zélie, in true hipster fashion of every Catholic mom who receives terrible quips about her family size, responded, "I didn't think that the sorrows and worries could ever be weighed against the eternal happiness of my children."[3] While she grieved heartily and heavily for her children, she was never defeated, knowing "there is always joy alongside the pain."[4] She wrote to her sister about the matter, saying, "It is a great good to have a child in heaven, but it is not less painful for our human nature to lose the child; these are the great sorrows of our lives."[5] She even taught her living children to ask for their siblings in heaven to intercede for them, which they did, and many graces were procured.

Zélie was a hidden hipster—one of those who preferred for herself and her family to be in the light of God's presence but out of limelight. It's no wonder that God chose to exalt this humble woman (see Matthew 23:12). And it's no wonder that St. Thérèse is known for her "little way." She first learned it from her mom, who did little, everyday things in both the joys and sufferings with great love.

### COOL SAINT
## VENERABLE LÉONIE MARTIN

Although she has not been canonized *yet*, this older sister of St. Thérèse of Lisieux has been named "Venerable" since her cause for beatification and canonization was opened in 2015. Léonie died at the age of seventy-eight in 1941 after being a Visitation nun for forty-three years. The third of nine children and the third of the five living sisters, she was considered the "difficult one" of the Martin sisters. She was seen as "untalented," with a temper, and her mother, Zélie, wrote in her letters about how worried she was over Léonie's sanctity. She was traumatically affected at a young age when her closest sister, Marie, died at the age of five. Then, it was discovered that the Martin family's maid of eleven years had been abusing her. That was a huge turning point, though, where she grew closer to her mom (who had been unaware of the abuse but fought like hell for her daughter when she discovered it). She continually brought Jesus into her wounds, and from her Visitation convent wrote, "I am very happy—as happy as it is possible to be on this earth. When I look back on my past, as far back as my earliest childhood, and compare that time with this, I am overwhelmed with gratitude to the Heart of Jesus, who has enveloped me in so much love, and who has placed me in this loveliest anteroom of heaven, where I shall live and die."[6] Her intercession has helped many others who have felt unwanted, forgotten, and troubled, especially in their families.

## FORGOTTEN PRAYER
# ACT OF RESIGNATION TO THE DIVINE WILL

O Lord my God, I now, at this moment, readily and willingly accept at your hands whatever kind of death it may please you to send me, will all its pains, penalties, and sorrows. Amen.

## LIVING THE FAITH

If you see a mom or a family with little kids at Mass, encourage them or lend any kind of help. When others are giving death stares or stank faces to the family with kids who are as energetic as squirrels, give a look of kindness and joy, and it may change their experience. You never know what a family is going through, and having others give encouragement is sometimes what keeps them Catholic!

# THE ART OF ACCOMPANIMENT: JOURNEYING WITH OTHERS IN FAITH

## Sr. Brittany Harrison, F.M.A.

When we consider the term "accompaniment," we may visualize helping an elderly person cross the street or holding a little girl's hand as she skips down the sidewalk. Accompaniment can seem like a mere supervisory activity rather than an expression of a relationship that leads both people toward Christ, but it's actually a very biblical way to grow in holiness with our friends and those whom we love.

In the Salesian spiritual tradition, borne of the spirituality of St. Francis de Sales and tailored for ministry with young people by St. John Bosco and St. Mary Mazzarello, accompaniment is an invitation to walk alongside others in their life journey, sharing their joys and sorrows, while also learning from their encounters with God how to deepen our own relationship with him. Accompaniment is not a one-sided, hierarchical dynamic; rather, it is a mutual expression of authentic friendship and love, desiring the good of another person and expressing true empathy and interest.

Since he was raised in a Salesian parish, Pope Francis understands this concept of accompaniment and wrote about it in his

135

encyclical *Evangelii Gaudium*: "The Church will have to initiate everyone—priests, religious and laity—into this 'art of accompaniment' which teaches us to remove our sandals before the sacred ground of the other (cf. Ex 3:5)" (169).

Our model of accompaniment is Jesus himself as seen in his encounter with the disciples on the road to Emmaus (see Luke 24:13–35). In reading this scripture, we find a perfect model of accompaniment as Jesus lays out the process for us:

1. Join—"Jesus himself came near and went with them" (Lk 24:15).
2. Dialogue—"And he said to them, 'What are you discussing with each other while you walk along?'" (Lk 24:17).
3. Explain—"Then beginning with Moses and all the prophets, he interpreted to them the things about himself in all the scriptures" (Lk 24:27).
4. Respect autonomy—"As they came near the village to which they were going, he walked ahead as if he were going on. But they urged him strongly, saying, 'Stay with us, because it is almost evening and the day is now nearly over.' So he went in to stay with them" (Lk 24:28–29).
5. Lead to Christ—All of this culminates in a eucharistic encounter with Christ in verses 30–35.

In accompanying the disciples, Jesus walked alongside them, listening to their troubles and identifying where they were in their journey. He invited them to share their experience and was receptive to hearing their interpretation of it. Realizing that they needed some guidance and clarification, he taught them in such a way that they were interested and not put off by this "stranger" being a know-it-all or haughtily reproving them, for he spoke as a friend who cared.

Accompaniment does not create an unhealthy dependence upon the accompanier. As the Emmaus journey progressed, Jesus did not force his continued presence on them, for true accompaniment cannot happen unless it is welcomed. He gave the disciples freedom to accept or reject his presence and waited for their invitation to continue with them. The disciples responded to the stranger, eager to continue with his friendship and guidance, and invited him to continue the conversation. Eventually the encounter revealed the presence of Jesus, in the stranger turned friend, through the Eucharist, which opened their eyes to the way God entered their story through this journey on the road.

When we accompany people, we are one way that Jesus touches the person we are journeying with. He uses us to guide and inspire, console and encourage. True accompaniment should instill in the accompanier a humble awareness of God working through him or her and a comfort in the one being accompanied, whom Christ is working through the relationship to draw to himself. The encounter with Christ through accompaniment is not one-sided but a dynamic experience for both the accompanier and the accompanied. Those who have been accompanied and those who accompany together rejoice in how God has operated in their lives and offer accompaniment to one another, as they witness to "what had happened on the road, and how [Christ] had been made known to them in the breaking of the bread" (Lk 24:35).

Accompaniment does not take place if it simply is reduced to a therapeutic relationship or a kind of narcissistic canonization process; there must always be a mutual journey toward God, a deepening of relationship with the Lord through friendship, sharing, challenging one another, and rejoicing in his presence. Pope Francis reminds us: "Spiritual accompaniment must lead others ever closer to God . . . to accompany them would be counterproductive if it became a sort of therapy supporting their self-absorption and ceased to be a pilgrimage with Christ to the Father" (*Evangelii Gaudium*, 170).

Accompaniment is not complicated, but it does demand selflessness, authentic love, and a sensitivity to how God works in our lives and the lives of those whom we care about. Perhaps we are already accompanying others without realizing it; perhaps we never had the vocabulary to explain this process that is seen in most healthy friendships. We all long for friendship, guidance, and a way to share our journey in faith. Accompaniment is a spiritual skill we can cultivate and, through it, encounter God in our lives and the lives of others.

## COOL SAINT
## ST. JOHN BOSCO

St. John Bosco lost his father when he was just a toddler. As a young boy, longing for accompaniment from a father figure who would help him figure out God's call in his life, he found it in a local priest, Fr. Calosso. This priest helped the young John Bosco to realize God's call to the priesthood and his invitation to be a father to the orphaned young people of Italy, turning his suffering into empathetic wisdom for the young.

## FORGOTTEN PRAYER
## PRAYER FOR ACCOMPANIMENT

St. John Bosco, father of young people and model of accompaniers, help me to transform my life experience, all of my sufferings and joys, into wisdom and insight for those whom I journey with in life. May I know the joy of the Holy Spirit working through me to lead others toward Christ as you did. Amen.

## LIVING THE FAITH

Create two lists. In one list, name all of the people who have accompanied you in your life, going back as far as you can remember. Identify how they have led you closer to God. In the second list, name the people whom you are accompanying or would like to accompany. Pray for people on both lists by name, thanking God for using them and you to be an extension of his presence.

# THE CATHOLIC WORKER ETHIC

## Tommy Tighe

Matthew, Mark, Luke, and John. The four gospels tell the story of Jesus Christ, God incarnate, the one who came to save each and every one of us from our sins. And yet, if that was *all* they did, they would actually fail in their mission.

The gospels aren't just a collection of stories for us to consume and continue on with life as if we'd never encountered them. Instead, they are a call to action. They were written to share what Jesus said and did while he was here on earth, sure, but their value comes from the fact that they inspire us, lead us to change our lives, and show us an example of how we are to work with the grace of God throughout the course of our days. One cannot help but read the gospels and feel compelled to action.

I've come to learn that this is the absolute highest praise that can be given to an author or creator of any other kind of media for that matter: "After I experienced your work, I knew I *had* to do something." This is the praise I heap on Servant of God Dorothy Day, cofounder of the Catholic Worker Movement and quite possibly the greatest modern example of leaving life behind to embrace the challenge of Jesus present in the gospels.

When I first picked up Dorothy's autobiography, *The Long Loneliness*, I really didn't know what to expect. Opinions on Dorothy and her life are pretty wide ranging among Catholics, and while I had read some of her articles from the Catholic Worker Movement website's archives, I really had no idea what I was getting myself into. I had absolutely no idea that within a week after finishing the book, I'd be taking my entire family to the Catholic Worker Hospitality House in Oakland, California, to get involved in the work, inspired by Dorothy's life.

That's what happened, though. I read *The Long Loneliness*, and I knew I *had* to do something.

I find it somewhat difficult to pin down what it was about Dorothy's life that inspired me just so dang much. Was it her down-to-earth writing style? Her life of struggling with sin despite knowing something more was out there? Her radical conversion? Her incredible ability to say yes to Jesus and his call to holiness even though the world seemed to offer something more appealing in the moment?

It was all of it, of course. All of it impacts our thinking and changes our way of life once we encounter it.

Dorothy once said, "The best thing to do with the best things in life is to give them up,"[1] and this countercultural philosophy of living simply, of embracing voluntary poverty in solidarity with the sisters and brothers around us who have no choice, is the idea I would like to hand directly off to all of you.

Of course, everyone has heard about Dorothy's work with the Catholic Worker Houses of Hospitality she cofounded, and everyone who reads about Dorothy's life and her work feels a certain fire within them, pushing them to want to move in the same direction. Reality can be very different. For me, as a father of a young family, it felt like something I could do every once in a while but not in a way that felt adequate to the fire growing within me. Thankfully, I found Dorothy's idea of voluntary poverty, something she brought into her life after getting to know Peter Maurin in New York, as a way for me to connect with my desire to help the poor even when I wasn't practically able to get over there to do so.

Giving up the good things in life on purpose, eating less because there are people in my very own town who have nothing to eat at all, not buying a new pair of shoes simply because there's a little hole in the bottom of the ones I have; all of these are *very* small sufferings to offer up for my sisters and brothers, to be sure, but it reminds me that there are so many in my town, my state, my country, and my entire world who have no choice but to go without. It reminds me to pray for them, work for them, and be more like them.

That's right, *be more like them.* Voluntary poverty isn't just about suffering for the sake of suffering; it isn't about giving things up just for the sake of simple living or being a minimalist. It's so much more than that. It's about literally learning to be poor and embracing all the spiritual growth that goes along with that life. Jesus said, "Blessed are the poor in spirit" (Mt 5:3), and the most effective way to move toward being poor in spirit is to work as hard as we can to alleviate the suffering of others while at the same time stripping away as many as possible of the conveniences and comforts present in our lives.

Voluntary poverty is also a great evangelization opportunity in a world that simply has no capacity for understanding why someone would strive to live in this way. When someone I come across asks why I would wear old-looking shoes that were ready to be replaced a few years ago, it's an opportunity to share with them exactly why I'm still wearing them. It's not because I'm cheap or lazy, it's not because I'm trying to look disheveled, and it's not that I don't care what other people think of me; it's because my sisters and brothers in Christ around the world have no choice, and I want to grow closer to them.

It isn't easy, especially when we've all be trained to want every new thing and always have the shiniest new cars, most delicious and trendy foods, and cell phone screens that don't have cracks in them (having a cracked screen and not forking over money to replace it is a great start, by the way). But for the sake of the poor, and for the sake of our souls, it would be worth it for you to explore Dorothy's life and writings, and see where they lead you.

## COOL SAINT
## SERVANT OF GOD DOROTHY DAY

Who else could it have possibly been?

Born in 1897 in Brooklyn, New York, Dorothy was inspired as a child growing up in Oakland, California, when she witnessed the incredible charity of others during the San Francisco earthquake of 1906. She was a social activist in her early adulthood and slowly converted to the Catholic faith over the years, culminating with the birth and baptism of her daughter, Tamar Teresa.

After praying for guidance in her life, Dorothy met Peter Maurin in New York, and the two would go on to change the world through their Catholic Worker Movement, which included a newspaper, houses of hospitality, and agrarian communities.

Despite once famously saying, "Don't call me a saint. I don't want to be dismissed so easily,"[2] Dorothy is most certainly on her way to becoming one of the most inspirational Catholic saints in the history of the United States.

Servant of God Dorothy Day, pray for us.

## FORGOTTEN PRAYER
## PRAYER FOR THE INTERCESSION
## OF SERVANT OF GOD DOROTHY DAY[3]

God our Creator,
your servant Dorothy Day exemplified the
Catholic faith by her conversion,
life of prayer and voluntary poverty,
works of mercy, and
witness to the justice and peace
of the Gospel.
May her life
inspire people
to turn to Christ as their savior and guide,
to see his face in the world's poor and
to raise their voices for the justice
of God's kingdom.

We pray that you grant the favors we ask
through her intercession so that her goodness
and holiness may be more widely recognized
and one day the Church may
proclaim her Saint.
We ask this through Christ our Lord. Amen.

## LIVING THE FAITH

Get on the internet and look up your closest Catholic Worker community. Get in touch with them, and tell them you'd like to help out in any way they want. They have many needs, and the incredible relationships you can build when directly helping the poor through the Catholic Worker are like nothing else you'll experience.

If there isn't one nearby, start taking stock of your life and honestly look into areas where you can cut back and embrace voluntary poverty. Start slow, and remember the reason for trying to live this way: not as a competition, not as a self-righteous Instagrammable act, but rather to live in solidarity with the poor, who are quite literally Jesus and should be taken care of as such.

# I'M NOT A REGULAR CATHOLIC; I'M A COOL (AND PRIDEFUL) CATHOLIC

## Julie Lai

If you're reading a book titled *Catholic Hipster: The Next Level*, this probably means you're cool. You're like Regina's mom in *Mean Girls* when she says, "I'm not a regular mom; I'm a cool mom." You're not like a regular Catholic; you're a cool Catholic. I get it. Your non-Catholic friends are probably a little shook that a Catholic could be this cool.

With all this coolness, I think it's good to be precautionary of Cool's lame brother that tends to tag along: Pride. Yep, good ol' pride. Pride for the cool hipster Catholic can look a little different. It can look like rolling your eyes every time someone says something liturgical that you disagree with. It can look like your identity being wrapped entirely in an aesthetic—you know, the whole image of, "Yeah, I'm Catholic, but I cuss sometimes, drink, and have tattoos." It could simply look like your life being so cool that you wonder if you really need the Lord in your life. Or perhaps doing another project or making another ministry that may or may not look pretty rad on your cause for canonization one day.

145

Pride is the antithesis of holiness. Holiness is the total and absolute dependence on Christ, while pride is self-reliant and self-absorbed. In other words, there is not room for both God and me on the throne of my heart. The Lord told St. Faustina, "The greatest misery does not stop Me from uniting Myself to a soul, but where there is pride, I am not there."[1] If you're at all cool and you know it, you will have to fight harder than anyone else to become holy.

The desire to be cool comes from two places. One, our good desire to be known. But two, our good and holy desire to simply be great. Our hungry hearts long to be seen and known. We know that it is only the Lord who can ultimately fulfill this desire. But we forget. We distort this good desire and say, "I'm not being self-seeking! I'm doing this for the Church!" or "I have to break every mainstream idea of what a Catholic looks like so more people will come to the faith!" Pride is sneaky in that way. Another way pride comes is through our desire to be great. As everyone's favorite quote from Benedict XVI notes, "You were made for greatness." It becomes quite problematic, though, when greatness through the world's standards is defined by originality, financial success, and popularity. The world drives us to climb up social ladders, but the Lord gives us the opposite model: of climbing *down* the social ladder to meet the lowly. The pursuit of vanity and pride is empty. But the pursuit after the Lord's heart gives us everything we could ever long for.

## COOL SAINT
## ST. AUGUSTINE

St. Augustine wrote extensively on pride and humility, and it led me to believe that he knew so much about this topic because it was probably the issue that he wrestled with most in his life.

Before his conversion, St. Augustine's life was wrapped up in his big reputation in academia, partying, drinking, and sex. He was caught up in seeking happiness in worldly things, only later to realize that he was truly seeking the Lord in these places. St. Augustine eventually had a major conversion through conversations with St. Ambrose and the reading of scripture.

Even after St. Augustine realized that truth was found in the Lord and the Catholic Church, however, he still wrestled with pride. He honestly said, "Lord, make me chaste, but not yet." He desired purity and holiness, yet he struggled with giving Christ the reins of his heart.

He eventually did choose chastity for his life. However, St. Augustine reminds me that the fight against pride is a daily one and not one that is slain overnight, even for the bravest of saints. Within a span of several years, St. Augustine was baptized, ordained a priest, and then ordained a bishop. His theological writings were groundbreaking. Despite these good things he was doing, he warned us against the distortion of doing good for our own pride. He said, "We have to fear pride even when we do right. We mustn't let our desire for praise cost us the things we do that are worthy of praise."[2]

St. Augustine gives us a beautiful example of humility because he fought against pride at each stage of his life. He reminds me that that I have to surrender my belief that my happiness lies in human accolade and the fulfillment of whatever my desires are. He reminds me that if I ever want to get over a certain sin in my life, I can't do it on my own. He reminds me to be cautious about my desire for praise. As St. Augustine said, "If you should ask me what are the ways of God, I would tell you that the first is humility, the second is humility, and the third is humility."[3]

### FORGOTTEN PRAYER
## LITANY OF HUMILITY

OK, FINE, the litany of humility is a pretty popular prayer. But if it's too popular for you to pray it, then you might just want to consider praying it twice. If it helps you can even remix it, like Tommy Tighe did: "From the desire to be retweeted, deliver us Lord."[4]

O Jesus! meek and humble of heart, Hear me.
From the desire of being esteemed,
Deliver me, Jesus.
From the desire of being loved . . .
From the desire of being extolled . . .
From the desire of being honored . . .
From the desire of being praised . . .
From the desire of being preferred to others . . .
From the desire of being consulted . . .
From the desire of being approved . . .
From the fear of being humiliated . . .
From the fear of being despised . . .
From the fear of suffering rebukes . . .
From the fear of being calumniated . . .
From the fear of being forgotten . . .
From the fear of being ridiculed . . .
From the fear of being wronged . . .
From the fear of being suspected . . .
That others may be loved more than I,
Jesus, grant me the grace to desire it.
That others may be esteemed more than I . . .
That, in the opinion of the world,
others may increase and I may decrease . . .
That others may be chosen and I set aside . . .
That others may be praised and I unnoticed . . .
That others may be preferred to me in everything . . .
That others may become holier than I, provided that I
  may become as holy as I should . . .

## LIVING THE FAITH

Do things that directly contradict the things you feel pride in. For example:

1. Ditch your hipster neck scarf and wear the clothes in your closet that you never wear.
2. Fast from social media for two weeks.

3. Do good for someone without them noticing it or telling anyone about it afterward—like, cleaning the kitchen at your workplace or secretly buying someone a nonfat, oat-milk, fair-trade, light-iced coffee.
4. If you're in a group setting, instead of talking to that cute gal/dude, talk to the person who is more reserved and perhaps not as attractive to you.
5. When you have a decision to make, ask yourself: What does pride want? What does humility want?

# THE CATHOLIC IDEA
# THAT'S KEY TO GENDER EQUALITY

### Samantha Povlock

I think it's safe to say that the Catholic Church is not regarded as particularly "progressive" for its teaching on birth control.

Condemning the thing that's supposed to free women to be equal to men? Not going to win you any feminist awards. But a college history class caused me to question that, and wonder: What if the Church held the key to true gender equality?

That semester in my history class—called "The History of Sexuality in America"—I learned about all the different ways that women have been discriminated against and taken advantage of for their biological vulnerability. Women's capacity to get pregnant is an incredibly vulnerable aspect of our difference and creates the opportunity for women to be raped and left pregnant, fired from their jobs for becoming pregnant, or left to suffer through difficult pregnancies or deliveries alone if they lack the necessary support. The emotional highs and lows women sometimes experience due to their cyclical hormones have been used frequently to discredit women's ability to be competent leaders or decision makers, and it's even been used to belittle our right to be respected in our opinions.

Because a woman's body appeared to be the source of all this vulnerability—and the source of all this oppression—many secular feminists began to focus on campaigning for an attitude of gender neutrality. The goal was to demonstrate how women weren't in fact that much different than men and, therefore, deserved to be recognized as fully equal to men. Birth control is the perfect tool through which to attempt to achieve this kind of equality, because it allows women to—with regard to fertility anyway—appear to imitate men's bodies.

"Women can be equal!" they said. "We can do everything men can do! We can be just like men if you promise to let us sit at the table."

And we have seen enormous progress for women in the workplace—at least, progress from where we were before—but take note, that progress disappears when we include women who are mothers. In fact, whether or not a woman is a mother has been shown to be the key factor in the pay gap.[1] And I can't say I'm shocked. The United States is still the *only* major developed country that doesn't offer mandated paid maternity leave.[2]

If you or someone you know has given birth, you know this is not a luxury we're asking for. Giving women time to recover from a major medical event is a serious medical need. It's a matter of justice.

But it's harder to fight for those rights when you've already bargained for "sameness" between the sexes. Here we see how the "My Body, My Choice," movement has quickly devolved into "Your Body, Your Choice, Your Problem." The failure to acknowledge women's biological differences has freed corporations, politicians, and society at large from accommodating women's very real medical needs in and outside of the workplace.

It doesn't stop there. This attitude has crept into our relationships, even our marriages. You see, the main "difference" between men and women is that women carry and bear children, and the way our bodies are designed and function is largely oriented around this capacity. The increasing forms and prevalence of birth control have seemingly enabled women to live and work side by side with men in all the same ways without having to worry about or make accommodations for pregnancy, childbirth, and everything that comes with them, such as breastfeeding. The problem is that this apparent state of "equality" for women still hinges on us censoring our difference—our capacity to get pregnant. Oh and sometimes, birth control fails. So then women's equality actually hinges not on birth control but on abortion.

So even with birth control, and abortion, women are left to deal with fertility on their own. That doesn't sound like equality to me, which is why this is one area where I think the Church is way ahead of the game.

You all know Catholics don't support using birth control, but do you know what they suggest using instead? It's called NFP—natural family planning. Secular versions are often called Fertility Awareness Methods. NFP is any system in which people chart different physical signs of a woman's body so they can identify the few days each month when a woman is fertile. If they're trying to avoid pregnancy, they can then avoid having sex on those days.

Practicing NFP is not just a day-to-day awareness of whether or not it's a fertile day. The process of learning NFP requires men to learn how a woman's body functions and how different it is from their own. That knowledge is powerful. Just ask any man who's learned it. Not to mention, learning NFP is oriented around educating people on how women work. Honestly, how often can we say that's the case elsewhere?

NFP sets the tone that sex is different for women, and it serves as a constant reminder to both men and women that sex includes a kind of vulnerability for women that it doesn't require from men. NFP is feminist because it invites men back into the conversation on fertility. It invites men to be equally aware of and responsible for what can happen when you have sex, and it demands men be equally intentional about their actions.

Now, some of you might be wondering—can't all this be true with birth control, too?

Not quite.

NFP is not just "Catholic approved" birth control—and that is a really important distinction. People may try to use NFP methods as just a "natural" contraceptive, but without discernment, it's not actually NFP. The purpose and power in NFP is the constant discernment and conversation between spouses. The Church says that whether a couple wants to get pregnant or avoid pregnancy, they need to discern it, discuss it, and then consciously choose their actions accordingly. This is why if people use NFP but aren't communicating or a husband resents or blames his wife for her cycle, something needs to change. Because that's not mutually taking responsibility; it's still the woman bearing the burden of fertility by herself.

The more men learn about NFP, the more empowered they are, too. Because they can see for themselves their wives' cycles are changing and what to expect based on what the couple has discussed. They can also better support their wives through their erratic cycles, PMS, or challenges conceiving. But they need the knowledge to do so.

For too long, men's bodies and the way they work has been upheld as the "gold standard." Birth control sustains this idea by providing women "equality" through attempting to conform their bodies to this standard, which leaves women alone as responsible to control their fertility and deal with the ramifications of it. But St. John Paul II said we need a feminism that rejects this idea of women imitating—or conforming—to be just like men.

True equality requires that we first acknowledge how women's bodies work and then we invite men to be equally aware of how fertility works as a couple. That's exactly what NFP does. And that's what a Catholic teaching on equality says. Women need to stop merely trying to imitate men and to stop being ashamed of how their bodies work or thinking of themselves as a burden. And as a culture, we need to ask more of men and stop underestimating them.

Ladies, it's time to invite men into this part of our selves, our lives, and our relationships. Men, we need you to be open and willing, ready to learn and ready to take an active role in fertility.

It's what the Church is calling you to do in the name of justice, and equality.

## COOL SAINTS
## STS. LOUIS AND ZÉLIE MARTIN

Both St. Louis and St. Zélie wanted to take religious vows but were rejected for education and health reasons, respectively. They later met and married, intending to remain celibate until a spiritual director counseled them that their marriage should be open to life.

The couple went on to give birth to nine children, with only five living past infancy or early childhood. Each of those five daughters became nuns, including St. Thérèse of Lisieux, one of four female Doctors of the Church.

Both of these saints ran their own businesses—Louis was a watchmaker and Zélie was a lace maker. After Zélie's lace-making business became very successful, Louis sold his watchmaking business to go into partnership with her. Their letters reveal the deep love and respect the couple had for each other and the beautiful witness of both complementarity and equality in marriage.

## FORGOTTEN PRAYER
## PRAYER OF SPOUSES AND PARENTS TO STS. LOUIS AND ZÉLIE MARTIN

Sts. Louis and Zélie Martin,
today we turn to you in prayer.

By fulfilling the duties of your state in life
and practicing the evangelical virtues
as spouses and as parents,
you have modeled for us
an exemplary Christian life.

May the example
of your unwavering trust in God
and your constant willingness to surrender
all the joys, the trials,
the sorrows and the sufferings
that filled your life
encourage us to persevere
in our daily challenges
and to remain in joy and Christian hope.
Amen.

## LIVING THE FAITH

Start with learning about the biological differences between men and women's bodies—in our brains, our hormones, and even the ways drugs interact differently with our bodies. Learn as well about the different methods of NFP and the different signs in a woman's body that are able to be charted.

Read stories of couples who use NFP and how it has impacted their relationships. Talk to other Catholic friends about their experience using, or not using, NFP. Don't be afraid to acknowledge the challenges that exist with NFP, and consider: What needs to be done here to help? More research, better promotion, more community support?

Whether you are male or female, single or married, pray about whether you see the female body as "limited" or "less than ideal" in the way God designed it. If you don't already see it as a gift, pray that God may reveal the goodness of his designs to you.

# HOW TO MAKE A FLANNERY O'CONNOR PILGRIMAGE

Fr. Damian Ference

There are three things that can really help you mature as a Catholic Christian; they are prayer, study, and travel. Making a Flannery O'Connor pilgrimage involves all three.

If you are not familiar with Flannery O'Connor, here's a brief biography: Mary Flannery O'Connor was born on March 25, 1925—the Feast of the Annunciation—in Savannah, Georgia, and was raised by her devout Catholic parents, Edward and Regina. An only child, O'Connor took to reading and writing at a very young age and was especially inspired by the stories of Edgar Allan Poe. Her father died of lupus when she was a teenager, and she and her mother moved to Milledgeville, Georgia, where she studied at the Georgia College for Women. After graduating, she earned an MFA at the University of Iowa Writers' Workshop; it was during her time in Iowa that O'Connor decided to drop the "Mary" from her name in order to avoid prejudices of being a female writer in the 1940s. O'Connor then headed to New York and was part of the Yaddo artists' community for some time and eventually moved to Connecticut with her dear friends, the Fitzgerald family. In 1951, she was diagnosed with lupus and moved back to Milledgeville, living on a 544-acre family farm, Andalusia, with her mother. Every morning after Mass and breakfast, O'Connor devoted her entire morning to writing her fiction and essays. In the afternoon she would welcome visitors, tend to her peacocks (she had more than forty of them), read, go to doctor's appointments, and write letters to friends. After reading Thomas Aquinas for twenty minutes every night, she would retire at nine o'clock. O'Connor was thirty-nine years old and at the height of her writing powers when she died on August 3, 1964. She is known as America's greatest Catholic writer.

So why make a Flannery O'Connor pilgrimage? Because Catholics have been making pilgrimages for the past 2,000 years and because Flannery O'Connor was a devout Catholic. Also, strange and beautiful things happen on a Flannery O'Connor pilgrimage.

Before you begin your pilgrimage, you'll have some preliminary work to do. You don't have to read O'Connor's entire canon, but you should be familiar with her work. She wrote two novels, thirty-two short stories, about one hundred book reviews for her diocesan newspaper, a collection of essays, a prayer journal, and many, many letters, most of which are contained in the book *Habit of Being*. You ought to at least read the stories "A Good Man Is Hard to Find," "Parker's Back," "Good Country People," and "Revelation" before hitting the road. You may also want to watch the documentary *Uncommon Grace: The Life of Flannery O'Connor* by Beata Productions, which is an excellent introduction to O'Connor's life and work.

I recommend setting aside at least two full days to make a Flannery O'Connor pilgrimage, not including travel days. I would also recommend that you bring some good music for the journey, especially by artists who have been directly influenced by Flannery O'Connor. These artists include but are not limited to Bruce Springsteen, Lucinda Williams, Josh Ritter, Sufjan Stevens, Mary Gauthier, and U2. And although there is no evidence of a direct O'Connor influence, the music of Gillian Welch and Patty Griffin are always appropriate for a Flannery O'Connor pilgrimage.

The first stop of your Flannery O'Connor pilgrimage should be St. John the Baptist Cathedral on 222 East Harris Street in

Savannah, Georgia. This beautiful gothic cathedral is where Flannery entered into the life of grace through Baptism in 1925. The cathedral is open for self-guided tours Monday through Saturday. If you call the cathedral office in advance, you can arrange for a docent to lead you on a tour. Don't miss the stunning stained-glass windows that must have stirred the religious imagination of O'Connor in her formative years of childhood and adolescence. My recommendation is to tour the cathedral on Friday at 11:00 a.m. and then stick around for the noon Mass.

Your second stop in Savannah is only a two-minute walk from the cathedral. After Mass, walk down the cathedral steps and turn left, making your way around the perimeter of Lafayette Square to 207 East Charlton Street, the childhood home of Flannery O'Connor. In recent years, gifted members of the Savannah College of Art and Design restored this home, and their work is highly commendable. Much of the furniture and house décor is from the O'Connor family, and that which is not remains true to the time period. The living room and kitchen are on the first floor, along with many photographs of O'Connor, as well as her childhood library. Flannery's bedroom is upstairs on the back side of the house, and her parents' bedroom looks out onto Lafayette Square, literally in the shadow of the cathedral. As you walk by the bathroom at the top of the staircase, the tour guide will likely tell you the story of Flannery hosting playdates with her friends, in which she made them sit in the bathtub while she read her stories to them. After the tour you may want to pick up some O'Connor books, stickers, postcards, or whatever they are selling in the little gift shop that day. The Flannery O'Connor Childhood Home is open every day except Thursday.

If you can find a reasonably priced hotel in historic Savannah, book one. And if you can afford a good meal in Savannah, my favorite two restaurants are The Plantar's Tavern (23 Abercorn Street) and Huey's (115 East River Street); they are perfect places to discuss all things Flannery.

After a good night's sleep in Savannah, you'll make the drive to Milledgeville, which takes about two and a half hours. If you have any audio recordings of O'Connor's fiction, a good time to hear a short story or two is during this drive.

There are four major Flannery-related things to see once you arrive in Milledgeville. You can visit them in any order you wish, but here's what I recommend: Begin at the Flannery O'Connor room at Georgia College located at the North Clarke Street entrance to the library. There you will find her baptismal gown, her typewriter, and all sorts of books, quotes, and memorabilia. (O'Connor's personal library is also located at Georgia College, but access is limited to scholars.)

After visiting the Flannery O'Connor Room, you can walk or drive less than a mile to Sacred Heart Catholic Church, Flannery's home parish, at 110 North Jefferson Street. The church has been renovated since the Second Vatican Council, but there are pictures hanging along the back wall that will give you a sense of what it looked like when O'Connor was a parishioner. Flannery was a daily communicant, and although she wasn't always a fan of her pastor's preaching, she was devoted to the sacramental life of the Church and often told people that she wrote the way she did because she was Catholic. The parishioners of Sacred Heart are used to seeing Flannery pilgrims at their parish, and some of the older ones may even have a story to tell you about her. I once met a man who served her funeral Mass when he was a boy.

Next, you'll drive about four miles outside of town to Andalusia (2628 North Columbia Street), the home of Flannery O'Connor from 1951 to 1964. You won't be able to see the farmhouse from the main road, but there will be a sign to welcome you. The dirt road to her house is what you would expect it to be if you're familiar with O'Connor's stories, and when the white house with the red brick steps and matching tin roof come into view, you'll know that you've arrived. The farmhouse was restored in 2018 and is now in the custody of Georgia College.

The first time I visited O'Connor's home I knelt and wept at the threshold of her bedroom, which also served as her writing room. It's holy ground indeed. There's a lot to see in the house itself, but you don't want to miss the views from the iconic front porch. You'll see what she wrote about in so many of her stories from that porch, especially in terms of landscape and skyscape. And if you walk around the house to the barn on the back of the property, you'll know exactly why I encouraged you to read "Good Country People" the moment you see the two-story barn. There are peacocks at Andalusia again, but don't expect the male to show off his tail to you. They are stubborn birds. If you have time, you might want to sit on one of the many rocking chairs on the front porch and read a story, an essay, or at least a few of O'Connor's letters before you leave. Flannery O'Connor took her vocation as a writer most seriously, and it's worth spending some time considering the seriousness of your own vocation before you leave Andalusia.

Your final stop in Milledgeville will be Memorial Hill Cemetery where Flannery O'Connor's body is buried. There is a map in a gazebo near the front gate of the cemetery, which indicates the location of her grave, and it's not hard to find. Take your first left upon entering the cemetery and walk down about eighty yards or so and then take another left toward the front fence and you'll walk right over to the O'Connor-Cline section of the cemetery. There you will find Flannery O'Connor's tombstone next to those of her mom and dad and other family members. I think Flannery O'Connor likely did some time in purgatory, but I've been counting on her intercession for some time now, so when I visit her grave, I always ask her to pray that I write well, especially if I'm writing about her. I'm not going to tell you what to pray for while you visit her grave, but I will tell you that she's a powerful intercessor.

If you stay in Milledgeville that night, The Brick (136 West Hancock Street) and Aubri Lane's (3700 Sinclair Dam Road) are my favorite places to eat and discuss the gift of Flannery O'Connor to the Church and the world. You can also find some very affordable hotels near Andalusia, just outside of town, but if you have the resources, the Antebellum Inn is a nice little bed and breakfast in town, and they have a great pool and offer a good breakfast.

To date, I have made five Flannery O'Connor pilgrimages with five different groups of people. Each one has been different, but each one has helped me mature as a man, as a Catholic, and as a priest. If you decide to make a Flannery O'Connor pilgrimage, it'll make you a better Catholic than you already are. And if you're not already Catholic, you'll want to become one by the end of your pilgrimage. Cheers!

## COOL SAINT
## ST. JOHN THE BAPTIST

There are a lot of saints who remind me of Flannery O'Connor, but St. John the Baptist, the voice crying out in the desert, is hard to top. Recall that O'Connor was baptized at St. John the Baptist Cathedral in Savannah, and also note that the title of her second novel, *The Violent Bear It Away*, comes from Matthew 11:12: "From the days of John the Baptist until now, the kingdom of heaven suffereth violence, and the violent bear it away" (Douay-Rheims).

St. John the Baptist suffered a violent death, and Flannery O'Connor wrote violent fiction, not for the sake of violence but to shock her reader into paying attention to God's grace breaking through and into the lives of her characters.

## FORGOTTEN PRAYER
## FLANNERY O'CONNOR PRAYER JOURNAL[1]

> Please let Christian principles permeate my writing and please let there be enough of my writing (published) for Christian principles to permeate.

## LIVING THE FAITH

Block out a few days in your calendar in the coming year and make a Flannery O'Connor pilgrimage.

# CATHOLIC BEES

## Haley Stewart

What's more Catholic hipster than bees? Stick with me here. Bees pop up in the liturgy, they are a spiritual metaphor, candles used for worship must be made of beeswax, and we've got beekeeper saints. Bees, y'all!

Even though beeswax is no longer the only option for candles, liturgical candles are required to be at least 51 percent beeswax. Why? It burns clean instead of smoking and leaving residue, and it has a pleasing scent. But beyond that, there is beautiful symbolism in the charity of the bees. St. John Chrysostom said in one of his homilies, "The bee is more honored than other animals, not because it labors, but because it labors for others."[1] Bees work in harmony, as we should. And they don't just work for the good of their sisters in the hive; bees also provide us with beeswax and sweet honey!

Every Easter Vigil, my beekeeping husband and son love to hear the Exsultet in the liturgy that talks about the Easter candle and the bees who made its wax:

> On this, your night of grace, O holy Father,
> accept this candle, a solemn offering,
> the work of bees and of your servants' hands,
> an evening sacrifice of praise,
> this gift from your most holy Church.

But now we know the praises of this pillar,
which glowing fire ignites for God's honour,
a fire into many flames divided,
yet never dimmed by sharing of its light,
for it is fed by melting wax,
drawn out by mother bees
to build a torch so precious.

So we worship with the help of bees, we honor them for their selfless labors, and bees just might be particularly pious creatures. There have been many cases when an icon is inserted into a hive and the bees cover it with comb except for the face of Our Lord or a saint. Could there be another explanation for this other than the bees' piety? Maybe, but I'm on Team Devout Bees.

Saints with a special affinity to bees include St. Gobnait and St. Ambrose. St. Gobnait (feast day February 11) was a sixth-century Irish nun who kept bees that would follow her command to attack invaders in order to protect the convent where she was abbess. St Ambrose, the bishop of Milan (feast day December 7), was visited by bees as a child. They covered his face, leaving a drop of honey to represent his preaching ability, leading him to be called "the honeyed-tongued preacher."

## COOL SAINT
# BL. SOLANUS CASEY

Bl. Solanus Casey was a twentieth-century American Capuchin friar who became the porter at St. Bonaventure Monastery in Detroit, Michigan. He felt called to the priesthood but struggled in his studies, and so he was urged to join a religious order to become a simplex priest (a priest who could celebrate Mass but not preach or hear confessions). He offered Masses for the sick, and his spiritual counsel was highly sought after. He loved the violin and worked miracles, including a particularly delightful multiplication of ice cream cones. He had a special connection with the monastery bees and could calm an angry hive with just the sound of his voice.

## FORGOTTEN PRAYER
## BLESSING OF THE BEES[2]

Lord God, Almighty, who didst create heaven and earth, and all the animals that live in the air and on the earth for the use of man; Thou who hast directed that the ministers of thy holy Church should light candles made of beeswax when the holy sacrifice is offered in which the Sacred Body and Blood of Jesus Christ, thy Son, becomes present and is consumed; send down thy blessing on these bees, that they may multiply and be fruitful and be preserved from all harm so that the product of their labor may be used to thy honor, and to the honor of thy Son, and the Holy Spirit, and the most blessed Virgin Mary. Through the same Christ our Lord. Amen.

## LIVING THE FAITH

Observe liturgical seasons such as Advent in your home with beeswax candles, remembering the symbolism of the bee. Support your local beekeeper by getting your honey and candles straight from the source. Or better yet, find a group of beekeepers who will teach you to keep a hive of your own!

# NFP, YEAH YOU KNOW ME

## Tommy Tighe

Typing on the computer, the doctor asked a question we had heard many times before: "So, what method of contraception do you use?" My wife and I shared a glance, knowing exactly where this interaction was headed. My wife answered in an almost whisper, "Natural family planning."

The doctor's puzzled response made it hard to know if he truly didn't hear what she said, or just couldn't believe what was said: "What's that?"

"Natural family planning," we both responded.

"Mmm . . ." was the doctor's response as he turned back to the computer and started typing, undoubtedly putting a note into our chart that said something like "Crazy Catholics."

Okay, that last part may just be my mind running wild simply because the situation was awkward, but those interactions at the doctor's office have never been easy. And that's only *one* of the situations where you take a moment to ask yourself the question *everyone* who practices NFP eventually asks themselves: "Is this really worth it?"

The Church's teaching against the use of artificial contraception is generally understood to be one almost universally panned by Catholics in the pews, at least if you take polls as an indication of sincerely held beliefs and practices. Despite that, the Church has held fast to the teaching most succinctly presented in the papal encyclical *Humanae Vitae* from St. Paul VI back in 1968.

Stating the teaching as simply as I can, the Catholic Church stands against artificial contraception because it thwarts the way God made us, disrupts the ability to give and receive the unconditional love we were made for, and renders the twofold purpose of intimacy broken. Conversely, the Church approves of natural family planning, perhaps more precisely called "fertility awareness," as it takes the natural information provided by God and refined through science to determine when a baby is likely to be conceived and when a baby is unlikely to be conceived, and then leaves it up to the couple to decide (through prayer, conversation, and careful discernment) what to do next.

We hear again and again from secular media and Catholic media alike that the teachings of the Church on this matter are widely ignored and the push from our culture to see this teaching of the Church as outdated and irrelevant has never been more intense. So why would anyone continue on with it?

First, and probably most important, because it's true.

What *Humanae Vitae* says about what happens in a relationship where artificial contraception is used will undoubtedly ring true for anyone who has found themselves in such a relationship (or anyone who is currently in such a relationship, as I was when I first picked up the encyclical). The way that intimacy slowly corrupts itself into being more about pleasure than giving and receiving that total gift of self was the one that hit me straight in the heart. When I took a good and honest look at myself, my thoughts, and where I was coming from in my relationship, I knew this was true and I knew I didn't like it. In the bigger picture, St. Paul VI made predictions about what would happen if the culture rejected *Humanae Vitae*, and all of his predictions have come true: a general lowering of moral standards, women being seen more as objects for use rather than persons deserving love and respect, a rise in marital infidelity, and governments seeing it as their role to encourage and, in some cases, force contraception on the public.

Hard to argue with that.

Second, and maybe the most powerful for evangelizing this teaching to other couples, is the impact that avoiding artificial contraception has on a relationship. When my wife and I decided to toss the contraception in the trashcan and start the journey of embracing the Church's teaching, we immediately noticed a change in our relationship. We slowly became more focused on each other, more interested in doing everything we could to show the other love, and closer and more intimate than we had been before. The Church points out that artificial contraception disrupts our ability to give and receive unconditional love on a deep emotional and spiritual level, and we saw that immediately in our own relationship when we pushed the contraception away.

That's why, no matter how hard it is, no matter how uncomfortable it might get in certain situations, no matter how weird it might make us look to the culture (and even to the majority of Catholics), we will never turn back. We have been there, we've left, and we've seen the light.

If you've had *even an ounce* of interest in the Church's teaching on this matter, *even a tiny bit of a thought* that it might be for you, check out *Humanae Vitae* (it's free online, after all). Give it a read, and be open to the Holy Spirit moving you in a direction that might feel crazy, scary, and uncomfortable.

It's totally worth it.

## COOL SAINT
## ST. PAUL VI

Who else could we highlight in a section about natural family planning but Giovanni Battista Enrico Antonio Maria Montini?

Pope Paul VI guided the Church through a very difficult time in the history of the world: a time of rejecting authority, the sexual revolution, and people moving away from religion and toward a more self-centered style of living. And yet, he guided it bravely.

He knew exactly the kind of backlash that would occur when he released *Humanae Vitae*, and he went ahead and did it anyway. He stood up for the truth when it was hard to do so, and all of us are experiencing the benefit of his guidance all these decades later (not to mention the children here today, enriching all of our lives, thanks to his message!).

He was canonized by Pope Francis in 2018, and now we can ask for his intercession for all of us trying hard to stick with the Church in the area of marital love and growing our families.

St. Paul VI, pray for us.

## FORGOTTEN PRAYER
## PRAYER OF POPE PAUL VI

Make us worthy, Lord, to serve our fellow men throughout the world who live and die in poverty and hunger. Give them through our hands, this day, their daily bread, and by our understanding love, give peace and joy. Amen.

## LIVING THE FAITH

If you are currently using artificial contraception (or even if you're not), go online and print yourself out a copy of *Humanae Vitae*. It's a short read, only thirty-one paragraphs, and it packs a serious punch. Allow the words of Pope Paul VI to sit with you for a little while, reflect on them, and see what they mean for you in your life. That's it. No pressure.

# CO-CREATING WITH GOD

## Theresa Zoe Williams

One morning on our drive to school, my kids were looking out the windows and declaring, of the things they could see, which things were created by God and which were created by man.

"God created the sky and the sun and the grass and the mountains," my daughter said, "but tires are created by people."

"But where did people get the materials to make tires?" I asked her. This started a conversation about what tires are made of, how we get those materials, and where those materials come from. Ultimately, we agreed that God made the materials needed to make tires and that people put those materials together to make them. God gives us all of the materials we need and we use them to create the items we need.

Humans are the only created beings who can also create, because we are created in the image and likeness of the Creator. Since he created us in his image and likeness, he imbues us with the power to create. We see this, perhaps most profoundly, in the creating of a new human life. Man and woman come together to create a new person, while God simultaneously acts to create a new, unrepeatable, immortal human soul and imbues the new human body with this soul. In this way, humans intimately act as co-creators with God.

But we are called to co-create with God in more ways than just creating new life. God gave human beings dominion over the created world—dominion to create names and purposes for everything of the earth and to use and create in ways that are in union with his will.

The concluding meditation of the Ignatian Spiritual Exercises is "Contemplation on the Love of God." There are four themes to reflect on in the meditation:

1. the gifts of God to us, such as life, family, faith, and eternal life
2. the self-giving of God in Jesus
3. the continuing work of God in the world
4. the limitless quality of God's love

The goal of the meditation is to recognize that in his love, God is in, upholds, and makes possible all things and that if God were to withdraw himself from something or someone, it would simply cease to exist. Creation is intimately wound up in God and completely dependent upon him for existence, which means that we are intimately wound up in God and completely dependent upon him for our existence.

At the end of the contemplation, we are invited to make a generous response of love to God in return and then go out into the world, see it anew, and live this profound love. The more we see ourselves and the world as gifts of creative and infinite love, the more we will wish to participate in this creative power as a response of love.

In this age, more and more people are returning to a creative life. Many people raise chickens or plant vegetable gardens. More people do freelance work as writers, editors, graphic designers, various types of consultants, or other such jobs. And many people have returned to making their own home goods such as clothes, jewelry, home decor, or the like; just take a look at Etsy to see that many have found their passions in this and are making a living doing so. Celebrated Catholic writer Flannery O'Connor understood this well. In her prayer journal she wrote, "Dear God, tonight it is not disappointing because You have given me a story. Don't let me ever think, dear God, that I was anything but the instrument for Your story—just like the typewriter was mine."[1]

So we are all meant to participate in creation with God. Catholic artist Cory Heimann of Likable Art put together a book of reflections on just this purpose titled *Created: Bridging the Gap between Your Art and Your Creator*, filled with little wisdoms from contemporary Catholic artists. Painter Margherita Gallucci's little words of wisdom are "Participate in God's creative power." Another favorite of mine from the book is "Everything is (actually) spiritual," by filmmaker, photographer, and designer Dan Rogers.

"Beauty will save the world," Russian writer Fyodor Dostoyevsky wrote. Beauty created the world, the world was created in beauty, and mankind is meant to continue to bring beauty to the world by participating in God's creative role. Catholic hipsters are returning to humanity's creative roots through their art, lifestyles, careers, and outlook on the world. They know that God's love is displayed gloriously in his role as Creator, and they are taking their place beside him as co-creators. After all, the Bible does begin with the five words "In the beginning, God created" (Gn 1:1).

## COOL SAINT
## ST. CATHERINE OF BOLOGNA

St. Catherine of Bologna was born on September 8, 1413, in Bologna, Italy, to an aristocratic family. Her father was a diplomat to the Marquis of Ferrara, and he sent her to court when she was eleven to be a companion to the Marquis's daughter, Princess Margarita. Catherine and Margarita became good friends and received an excellent education in music, literature, painting, dancing, and other subjects. Catherine excelled at painting, Latin, and playing the viola.

When Margarita became engaged, she wanted Catherine to remain as her companion, but Catherine felt called to religious life. At thirteen or fourteen years old, Catherine joined a convent. A few years later, she and a few other young women of Ferrara founded a monastery of Poor Clares. She delighted in serving in the more humble roles in the convent, such as laundress, baker, and caretaker to the animals.

While in the convent, Catherine continued her artistic pursuits, playing the viola, painting religious images, copying and illuminating her breviary, and writing spiritual treatises and poetry. Her painting of St. Ursula now hangs in a gallery in Venice, Italy, and her breviary, which once belonged to Pope Pius IX, is now on display at Oxford University. One of her most renowned spiritual works is *The Seven Spiritual Weapons*. One of the weapons she describes is about trusting in God, for "alone we will never be able to do something truly good."[2] She knew that absolutely every portion of her existence was in complete dependence upon God!

When Catherine was forty-nine, she became gravely ill and died on March 9, 1463. As was the custom of the Poor Clares, she was buried without a coffin, just straight into the ground. Many cures were attributed to her at her gravesite, and a sweet aroma was recorded as permeating from her grave. Eighteen days after she was buried, her body was exhumed and found to be completely incorrupt! More than 600 years later, her body remains incorrupt (though her skin has been blackened due to exposure to oil lamps and soot). Her body is clothed in her religious habit and seated on a golden throne behind glass in the chapel of the Poor Clares in Bologna.

St. Catherine of Bologna is the patron saint of artists and the liberal arts because of her artistic pursuits and mastery. She is also patron against temptations. Pope Benedict XVI said of her, "From the distance of so many centuries she is still very modern and speaks to our lives. She, like us, suffered temptations, she suffered the temptations of disbelief, of sensuality, of a difficult spiritual struggle. She felt forsaken by God, she found herself in the darkness of faith. Yet in all these situations she was always holding the Lord's hand, she did not leave him, she did not abandon him. And walking hand in hand with the Lord, she walked on the right path and found the way of light."[3]

## FORGOTTEN PRAYER
## SUSCIPE BY ST. IGNATIUS OF LOYOLA

Take, Lord, and receive all my liberty, my memory, my understanding, and my entire will, all that I have and possess. You have given all to me. To You, O Lord, I return it. Everything is Yours; dispose of it wholly according to Your Will. Give me only Your love and Your grace, that is enough for me. Amen.

## LIVING THE FAITH

Find a way to live a more creative life—whether that be through crafting, home decorating, gardening, writing, or whatever else interests you. Pick one way you can be a creator and make time, even for just ten minutes, each day to practice this craft. And each time you do this activity, offer it to God and ask him to work with and through you to make his beauty manifest in the world.

# MAKING ALL THINGS NEW

## Matthew Sewell

I was baptized when I was eight weeks old. My family were weekly Mass-goers, Mom was the parish youth minister, Dad cooked all the Knights of Columbus pancake breakfasts, and I helped clear the church sidewalks in the winter from the time I could carry a shovel. As an altar server at the age of ten, a member of the diocesan youth council at fifteen, and an attendee of Catholic college at eighteen, I believed what the Church taught me was true and could reasonably hold my own in conversations (admittedly without much real depth) about all the "Catholic things." But I didn't know that prayer actually worked—that it could bear tangible fruit in the form of a healing of one's soul—until I was nearly twenty-seven years old. I didn't really believe that Jesus could manifestly act in my life to heal old wounds once and for all, as if the verse in Revelation—"See, I am making all things new" (21:5)—was just a pious platitude from a forgotten age.

It was only when a close friend reached out to me in the midst of my pending divorce that my eyes were opened. My friend had been regularly checking in with me, but with him being a seminarian, these check-ins happened typically later in the evening as he killed two birds with one stone by seeing how I was doing and simultaneously shirking an impending class deadline.

177

But one day he texted me out of the blue, mid-morning, and said, "I think you need to ask the Lord for what you want."

I responded, "Yeah, I'm pretty sure that's not how that works."

He replied, "No, really. My spiritual director is always talking about how the Lord wants to give us good things. If our hearts are properly disposed and aligned with his, then our petitions will be answered by God."

The verses from Matthew's gospel came to mind: "Is there anyone among you who, if your child asks for bread, will give a stone? Or if the child asks for a fish, will give a snake?" (7:9–10). So I humored him.

I discovered six days later that the Lord had answered the prayer—my then-wife was battling a chronic depression that not only was causing a temptation to self-harm but also prevented her from being able to focus clearly and decide affirmatively for her own happiness. The prayer, as I discovered, had borne the fruit of suddenly making these circumstances simply disappear.

In that moment, I realized that I had never before actually believed that prayer could "work," that the Lord desired good things for his children and was willing to give them if only we would ask for them. This experience, though not enough to save my marriage, was a catalyst in a months-long process of dialogue with the Lord and decisive healing of wounds I'd carried for decades.

Since the fall of Adam and Eve, we have been pining for a reunification with our Creator. Jesus Christ bore our sin to make that possible for us, once and for all. But our union with God is still dependent upon our choice to be with him. The prodigal son had to first choose to return to his father's house to be showered with the father's love. It was the son who never left who missed the point—all that he needed was right in front of him. All he had to do was see the father's gift and accept it.

In the Garden of Eden, God "created man in his own image" and was perfectly united with his creation before the Fall. Adam and Eve were *whole*. But the Fall did happen. "Sin is present in human history," as the *Catechism of the Catholic Church* tells us, and "any attempt to ignore it or to give this dark reality other names would be futile" (386).

Do we believe that Jesus Christ not only desires to heal us of that sin but *is capable* of healing us of our woundedness? Pope Benedict XVI once said that "healing is an essential element of . . . Christianity. . . . It expresses the entire content of our redemption."[1]

Dr. Bob Schuchts, in his landmark book *Be Healed*, notes the story in John's gospel of Jesus approaching a man who had been sick for thirty-eight years, and plainly asking him "Do you want to be healed?" or (translated another way) "Do you want to be well?" Reflecting on the strangeness of Jesus' words, given that the man obviously would want to be well, Schuchts notes: "[Jesus] must know something about the deeper paralysis of this man's soul that isn't immediately obvious to me. After all these years, it appears this lame man *has given up hope that he will ever be healed*. . . . After all these years of struggling with our various physical, psychological, and spiritual infirmities, have we somehow resigned ourselves to our broken condition?"[2]

Is it reasonable, at least, to believe that Jesus doesn't desire us to be broken, wounded disciples?

If we profess the unconditional love of God, why then do we put conditions upon the deepest desires of our hearts, refusing to ask him to heal us of our deepest hurts, much less believe that he would actually do it?

## COOL SAINT
## ST. RAPHAEL THE ARCHANGEL

St. Raphael the Archangel, known as the patron saint of healing, is typically remembered for appearing to Tobiah and his wife Sarah in the Book of Tobit. But few realize that it is Raphael who is referred to in John 5:4, the very same scene in which Jesus was talking to the sick man: "An angel of the Lord descended at certain times into the pond and the water was moved. And he that went down first into the pond after the motion of the water was made whole of whatsoever infirmity he lay under" (Douay-Rheims).

## FORGOTTEN PRAYER
## HEALING PRAYER OF SURRENDER (ABRIDGED)

Dear Lord Jesus, it is my will to surrender to you everything that I am and everything that I'm striving to be. I open the deepest recesses of my heart and invite your Holy Spirit to dwell inside of me.

I ask you to take Lordship over every aspect of my life. I surrender to you all my hurt, pain, worry, doubt, fear and anxiety, and I ask you to wash me clean.

I release everything into your compassionate care. Please speak to me clearly, Lord. Open my ears to hear your voice. Open my heart to commune with you more deeply. I want to feel your loving embrace. Open the doors that need to be opened and close the doors that need to be closed. Please set my feet upon the straight and narrow road that leads to everlasting life. Amen.

## LIVING THE FAITH

Next time you go to prayer, focus on *one thing* in your heart that you've never quite been able to shake. The one thing that's constantly nagging at you and that you might be telling yourself internally is always going to be a part of you. Have you invited the Lord into that? Have you asked him to heal it? Be bold, be vulnerable, and be welcomed into the Father's arms.

# ST. ANDREW, AN APOSTLE BEFORE IT WAS COOL

Patrick Neve

This story is going to sound extremely petty, but I need you to bear with me. When I was in high school, I came up with a goofy idea for a restaurant called Topical Smoothie, where all the drinks are named after current events. I was talking to a friend about it, and he told me he didn't think it was that funny. A few months later, that friend started a YouTube channel and one of the videos featured him talking about current events. The show was called *Topical Smoothie*. I am still upset about this.

For a hipster, the worst-case scenario is someone stealing your idea or copying your aesthetic, which is why I used this story to start talking about St. Andrew, the hipster apostle. I can't help but think that during one of the famous disciple-spats over who's the best, St. Andrew would have dropped the classic line, "I was here first!"

St. Andrew was originally a disciple of St. John the Baptist, but at the height of St. John the Baptist's popularity, he pointed St. Andrew and St. John the Apostle to Christ. After staying with Jesus for some time, St. Andrew finds his brother Peter and says, "We have found the Christ!"

Until college, I rarely gave much thought to St. Andrew. Besides the Scots and people named Andy, I have met very few devotees of his. However, I came across a Wednesday audience given by Pope Benedict XVI in 2006, discussing what we know about St. Andrew from scripture. In the gospels, Andrew evangelizes through mediation. He does this in three ways: Andrew brings Christ to others, brings others to Christ, and learns from the one Mediator.

Andrew had a unique and intimate relationship with Jesus. John recounts that he and Andrew spent several hours alone with Christ at the beginning of his ministry before the other apostles were called. Andrew shows this intimacy in Matthew 13, when he, Peter, James, and John question Jesus about the destruction of the temple. We should not be afraid to draw close to Jesus and ask him things we don't understand.

In John 6, at the multiplication of the loaves, St. Andrew is the one who points out the young boy with the barley and fish. He does so somewhat hopelessly, asking "What good are these for so many?" (6:9, NABRE), but he brings the boy to Christ anyway and thousands are fed. Sometimes evangelization feels like this. We see what little a person has and ask in our hearts, "What good is that?" Those are the very people the Lord wants to turn into great saints.

Later in John's gospel, shortly before the Passion, some Greek believers come to the apostles. Andrew and James both serve as interpreters for these men. Pope Benedict XVI points out that Andrew and James are two of the few apostles with Greek names. Tradition also teaches that Andrew was crucified in Patras, a city in Greece. The Greek Church has a great devotion to St. Andrew because of this.

Andrew had a desire to bring outside believers into the Church, and we should share this desire. In Matthew 12:30, Christ said to his apostles, "Whoever is not with me is against me," but in Mark 9:39, he said, "Whoever is not against us is for us." We need to reach out to Christians outside the Church who love Jesus and are open to full communion. In 1964, St. Paul VI returned a relic of Andrew to the Greek Orthodox Church as a gesture of ecumenism. Even after death, Andrew is still working to bring those outside of the Church inside.

The first person St. Andrew evangelized was his brother, Peter. Because of him, we have our first pope. Andrew doesn't get much attention in the gospels and isn't mentioned in Acts outside of the list of the apostles. Even still, the role he played was indispensable in building up the Church. When we answer the call to be fishers of men, we may not be remembered for what we do, but our work is necessary. The Church needs more Andrews.

## COOL SAINT
## ST. ANDREW

Because of St. Andrew's role as the Protoclete, pray a novena in preparation for Christmas. The novena begins on St. Andrew's feast day (November 30) and ends on Christmas Eve, and it involves praying the St. Andrew prayer fifteen times per day, every day leading to Christmas.

## FORGOTTEN PRAYER
## ST. ANDREW NOVENA PRAYER

Hail and blessed be the hour and moment in which the Son of God was born of the Most Pure Virgin Mary, at midnight, in Bethlehem, in the piercing cold.
In that hour, vouchsafe, I beseech thee, O Lord, to hear my prayer and grant my desire. Through the merits of Our Savior Jesus Christ and of His Blessed Mother.

## LIVING THE FAITH

Make a list of those closest to you in your life. One by one, pray about what you can do this week to reach out to them and love them better.

# ATTRACTION: HORMONES MEET THEOLOGY

## Jackie Francois Angel

Hipsters are always doing things before everyone else thinks they're cool. One of the greatest Catholic hipsters of all time was St. John Paul II. On the topics of sexual attraction, eros, and agape, weaving both psychology and theology, he was writing before anyone else. People in the realm of psychology, such as Sigmund Freud, were talking about the sexual urge in the early twentieth century. But Pope John Paul II chided Freud for saying that we are merely like animals with instinctual urges to which we are slaves. Today's psychologists have the benefit of knowing exactly which hormones are responsible for the sexual urge (testosterone and estrogen), attraction (dopamine and norepinephrine), and attachment (oxytocin and vasopressin), but they still don't have the depth and insight of the whole person and even the theology that Pope John Paul did almost sixty years ago.

In Pope John Paul II's book *Love and Responsibility* (written in 1960, when he was Cardinal Karol Wojtyla), he explains that while our sexual urges and attractions can be an initial starting point of love, we must not be enslaved to them but rather subordinate them to our intellect and will and integrate them to a greater love that wants the good for the other. For example, if I'm attracted to someone who is already taken, such as a married man or a priest, I may get a rush of testosterone, estrogen, dopamine, and norepinephrine in my body every time I see him and feel all the feels, like a unicorn exploding with glittery sprinkles. However, if I followed and acted on those feelings, or even became addicted to those feelings, I would be not loving that person and respecting their vows but becoming a slave to lust.

As one of my friends said, "Attraction doesn't have to *mean* something." What does that mean? Well, as humans, we are naturally attracted to that which is True, Good, and Beautiful. We *should* be attracted to other humans—their beauty, their goodness, their affirmation of the Truth. But we should appreciate others and love them like Christ, not use them and lust after them. Our attractions don't have to mean something more than just "Thank you God for this beautiful person!" Our attractions don't have to be sexualized. Our attractions don't have to mean that we should cheat on our vows or help others cheat on their vows. Being a Catholic, and especially a Catholic hipster, means that while everybody else is becoming a slave to hormones and feelings, we are becoming more integrated and allowing our feelings to be drawn into God's unconditional (agape) love. So, next time you find yourself attracted to someone, thank God for them!

### COOL SAINT
## ST. JOHN THE APOSTLE

St. John the Apostle and Evangelist was called "the Beloved Apostle" for his deep love and friendship with Jesus. Today people would call it a total "bromance," and again, you and I know that attraction doesn't need to be sexualized. St. John reclined on Jesus' breast at the Last Supper, and he was the only Apostle at the foot of the Cross. St. John wrote a lot about love, but one of my favorite examples of this is 1 John 4, where he writes, "Beloved, let us love one another, because love is of God; everyone who loves is begotten by God and knows God. Whoever is without love does not know God, for God is love" (1 Jn 4:7–8, NAB). Let us ask St. John to pray for us to have authentic love with all we meet, to be attracted to that which is true, good, and beautiful in every person, and to love as God has loved us. St. John, patron of friendship, pray for us!

## FORGOTTEN PRAYER
## A PRAYER OF ST. THOMAS AQUINAS

Dearest Jesus! I know well that every perfect gift, and above all others that of chastity, depends upon the most powerful assistance of Your Providence, and that without You a creature can do nothing. Therefore, I pray You to defend, with Your grace, chastity and purity in my soul as well as in my body. And if I have ever received through my senses any impression that could stain my chastity and purity, may You, Who are the Supreme Lord of all my powers, take it from me, that I may with an immaculate heart advance in Your love and service, offering myself chaste all the days of my life on the most pure altar of Your Divinity. Amen.

## LIVING THE FAITH

Put it into practice: the next time you are attracted to a person and are tempted to start fantasizing about them, simply pray, "Thank you, God, for their beauty. The end."

# HEROIC FRIENDSHIP

## Kaitlyn Facista

> No one has greater love than this, to lay down one's life
> for one's friends.
>
> —John 15:13

It seems to me that we've forgotten what friendship is supposed to look like. We're so busy rushing to school drop-off, work, church, our phones, and whatever show we're binge-watching, and our perfectly Instagrammable homes tucked away in gated neighborhoods, that we probably don't even realize how lonely we've become. *I haven't talked to my friends in weeks, but I've liked their tweets so that counts, right? I haven't invited anyone over in months, but I've posted photos of my clean kitchen on Instagram, so that counts, right? I'm comfortable right here on my couch, enjoying my locally brewed craft beer while I watch my favorite movie for the twentieth time. So that's enough, right?* we ask ourselves. Or maybe that's just me. But it's probably not.

Friendship is hard. It takes effort and time, it's inconvenient, it's uncomfortable, and sometimes it's scary. It's so much easier to ignore our coworkers, the other parents at our kids' school, or the people we're sitting beside at Mass than it is to reach out and try to form a connection. But the thing about that is it's a terrible idea. It's time to stop it. The whole rest of the world is becoming more and more individualistic, self-serving, and profit-driven, and when we adopt that mindset we lose sense of the value of friendship. But as Catholics, we are called to live with heroic friendship.

In John 15:12–15, Christ tells us, "This is my commandment, that you love one another as I have loved you. No one has greater love than this, to lay down one's life for one's friends. You are my friends if you do what I command you. I do not call you servants, because the servant does not know what the master is doing; but I have called you friends, because I have made known to you everything that I have heard from my Father." In these verses, we can begin to understand true friendship as Christ modeled it for us: by dying to our own selves for the sake of others. Friendship was never meant to be superficial or self-serving; rather, it was meant to be a gift of self we can give to others.

Opening yourself up to friendship begins with embracing a hospitality of the heart. And I don't mean the Pinterest-perfect dinner party sort of hospitality (unless that's your thing; then by all means go for it), but simply an attitude of welcoming and willingness to care for the people in your life. Hospitality is a state of mind and heart that isn't necessarily dependent on a person's home or resources. It doesn't matter if you're eating pizza off a paper plate on the floor of your studio apartment or serving a homemade meal from scratch in your four-bedroom home; a weary soul can find just as much comfort in one as in the other, as long as your time together is rooted in love.

To be honest, there have been a lot of times when I've avoided inviting people over to my house because of how messy it was. Sometimes I'm in a season of life when it's impractical to expect a clean house, such as when I've just had a baby or our whole family has been sick for two weeks straight, and that's fine. But there are other times when the house is a disaster simply because I haven't made its upkeep a priority. I think it's the same way with our hearts, too. If we want to be welcoming and open to caring for others, we need to take care of our hearts. This usually involves a lot of prayer, self-discipline, and a Christ-centered mindset. When we prioritize our relationship with Christ, we will be better able to nurture our other relationships. When we choose to care for the upkeep of our hearts and our homes (in whatever ways we are able), we are taking the first steps in making ourselves available for Christlike friendship to anyone who might need it.

In the eight years my husband and I have been married, we've moved thirteen times for his job. We've gone from rental to rental, staying in some places for a whole year or two and others for only a few months. Throughout all of our moves, I've struggled to form new friendships despite putting in what I felt like was a good effort. From my experience, by the time most people reach adulthood, they've already found their core set of friends and aren't necessarily motivated to make any more. If you fit this description, I hope you'll realize how blessed you are to have these solid friendships and that you'll make a conscious effort to welcome in new people as they come along. And if you're struggling to find a group of friends, I hope you won't lose heart and will continue to reach out to the people around you.

Because of how often we've moved, it has always been difficult to "make our home"— to fill it up, to make it look nice, to create the sort of environment we've wanted it to be. And I've often struggled with making home into an idol. We've jumped from rental to rental while I've watched my friends purchase their own homes, painting and decorating and putting down roots. I've longed for a home for a long time, but I'm beginning to see that the home I'm longing for is actually in heaven. Having this shift in perspective has really helped me when it comes to how I understand friendship and hospitality. Redirecting our mindset to our eternal home helps us become more willing to invite others into our hearts and homes on earth. Doing this has helped me to see that hospitality has nothing to do with the outward appearance and everything to do with the heart. There should be a welcomeness of the heart.

True friendship is always deeply rooted in love, the act of willing the good for another. How can we will the good of our neighbors? By being there for them. We can make ourselves available—mentally to hear about their days, spiritually to pray for them, or physically to invite them in for a meal or a drink. But without love, it means nothing. And this isn't always easy; in fact, it rarely is. Love is inconvenient, it's messy, it's uncomfortable—but it can also be our greatest joy.

Our neighbors are spiritually (and at times physically) starving, freezing, and homeless. Will we let them in? Will we feed them, clothe them, and offer them a place to spend an afternoon in friendship?

Let us comfort the sorrowful, guide the lost, feed the hungry, and offer a glimpse into the eternal peace of our Lord. This sort of life-giving friendship, this life-sustaining hospitality, is truly heroic.

> [Jesus said,] "Then the King will say . . . 'For I was hungry and you gave me food, I was thirsty and you gave me something to drink, I was a stranger and you welcomed me, I was naked and you gave me clothing, I was sick and you took care of me, I was in prison and you visited me.' Then the righteous will answer him, 'Lord, when was it that we saw you hungry and gave you food, or thirsty and gave you something to drink? And when was it that we saw you a stranger and welcomed you, or naked and gave you clothing? And when was it that we saw you sick or in prison and visited you?' And the king will answer them, 'Truly I tell you, just as you did it to one of the least of these who are members of my family, you did for me.'" (Mt 25:34–40)

## COOL SAINT
## BRIGID OF KILDARE

St. Brigid was born in Ireland around 451. She was the illegitimate daughter of a pagan chieftain and a Christian slave. When her father learned of her pregnancy, Brigid's mother was sold to another master with the intention of the child being returned to her father eventually. Brigid was raised Catholic and was a child of remarkable purity and generosity. One story from her childhood recounts that she was unable to eat or drink food given to her by her Druid master because of his impurity. When she was about ten, she was reunited with her father's family as a servant. Upon seeing her father's wealth, she was unable to resist giving generously to the poor. This enraged her father, who tried to sell her to the king, but the Christian king instead convinced her father to grant Brigid her freedom. Her father ultimately allowed her to become a nun, and her profession of vows was accepted by Bishop Mel of Ardagh—the nephew of St. Patrick. Along with St. Patrick, she is one of the patron saints of Ireland. Throughout her life, she was well-regarded by laypeople and clergymen alike for her wise counsel and mentorship. St. Brigid's life of generosity and authentic kindness can be an inspiration for all of us as we strive to be good friends to one another.

St. Brigid, pray for us!

## FORGOTTEN PRAYER
## PRAYER FOR GENEROSITY
## BY ST. IGNATIUS OF LOYOLA

Eternal Word, only begotten Son of God,
Teach me true generosity.
Teach me to serve you as you deserve.
To give without counting the cost,
To fight heedless of wounds,
To labor without seeking rest,
To sacrifice myself without thought of any reward
Save the knowledge that I have done your will.
Amen.

## LIVING THE FAITH

Go out of your way to be a good friend this week; do something inconvenient for friendship's sake. Pick up your phone and call someone you haven't talked to in a while instead of scrolling mindlessly through Twitter. Ask a friend to meet you for coffee instead of just grabbing your drink from the drive-thru. Remember that friend that you haven't seen in a year because they live forty minutes away? Make plans to go see them. Think about the people in your life who may be in a challenging season right now, struggling with a death in the family or the loss of a job, and be intentional about reaching out to them and helping in whatever way you can. Be flexible with your routine in whatever way you can to prioritize friendship over the things that don't truly matter. I promise you'll be glad you did.

# CONCLUSION

## Tommy Tighe

I'm a therapist in my daily life, and one of the things that most often comes up in my profession is that insight into one's issues doesn't necessarily make one feel better. Sure, it's good to get to the bottom of *why* you're feeling depressed, but then what? As a therapist, my job is to help people find practical ways to work toward healing, progress toward recovery, and take action rather than just make realizations.

I like to carry this line of thinking into how I approach my Catholic faith. Sure, it's great to know that Jesus died for me and my sins, but what does that mean for me? How am I supposed to act, given that understanding? How am I supposed to live my life in light of what I have learned through faith?

That is precisely the aim we tried to achieve with *Catholic Hipster: The Next Level*. We wanted to make sure we weren't simply leaving you with interesting ideas and realizations you may not have stumbled upon before. We wanted to make sure we were giving you an action plan, a way to direct your life toward giving yourself more completely to God and his Church.

From picking up new and powerful devotions, to considering a third order, to taking a stand for social justice, to accompanying those around you through a difficult time, the suggestions offered in this book have hopefully armed you with a list of things to get started on as you strive to deepen and strengthen your Catholic faith.

In an increasingly secular world, being Catholic is starting to feel like the only thing that makes any sense. And as we watch our own Church come to terms with its sins both past and present, we see more than ever before the importance of reflecting on our own holiness and making an effort to answer that universal call that God has offered to us all.

Consider this a promise that I will personally be praying for every single reader of this book, that the Holy Spirit will descend upon you, take you by the hand, and show you exactly where he wants to lead you.

Consider this a promise that I'll be storming heaven to intercede that all of us might get ourselves out of the way of and abandon ourselves to God so he can transform us into the saints he created us to be.

Consider this a promise that if I make it, I'll be looking for all of you up in heaven, eager to catch up on everything we've been through over an ice-cold craft beer.

Please pray for me and all the contributors to this awesome book, and join me in praying for all the readers so we can answer that universal call and have a giant party once we finally make it to the heavenly feast.

# ACKNOWLEDGMENTS

## Tommy Tighe

The fact that there now exists a sequel to *The Catholic Hipster Handbook* shocks me just as much as the original one getting published back in 2017! It's incredible to look back on the community we formed over in the Catholic corners of Twitter and see how far we've all come. We've been sharing our love of Christ, his Blessed Mother, and the Catholic faith, encouraging one another in the struggle to grow in holiness, and now actually having an impact on the Catholic media world like we always dreamed!

Huge props have to go out to the incredible team at Ave Maria Press. Can you believe they gave us *another* shot?! The entire team is so fantastically professional, helpful, and friendly, and I would highly recommend publishing a book with them if you're on the lookout.

Next up, I have to thank the real stars of this book: every single lovely contributor who made this book what it is. Kaitlyn Facista; Fr. Damian Ference; Jackie Francois Angel; Sr. Brittany Harrison, F.M.A.; Julie Lai; Patrick Neve; Samantha Povlock; Katie Prejean McGrady; Matthew Sewell; Haley Stewart; Holly Vaughan; and Theresa Zoe Williams deserve absolutely every single bit of credit for *Catholic Hipster: The Next Level*. Their writing is *vastly* superior to mine, and every contribution they provided inspired me to delve deeper and grow in love of my Catholic faith.

As much credit as the contributors deserve, however, this book seriously wouldn't exist without the love and support of my beautiful wife, Karen, and my unbelievably cute children. Poor Karen had to read over my contributions and gently and lovingly write all over them with a bright red pen. She always managed to do it with charity and compassion . . . and if my takes are any good at all, it's only because of her help.

Last but not least, thanks to all of you wonderful readers out there! I love you all, and I sincerely hope to meet you either here on earth or, better yet, up in heaven someday. I will honestly be praying for you all and ask that you pray for me as well!

# NOTES

### GUITARS AND ORGANS

1. Thomas Craughwell, *Heaven Help Us: 300 Patron Saints to Call Upon for Every Occasion* (New York: Chartwell Books, 2016), 291.

2. Matt Maher, "Adoration," *All the People Said Amen*, 2013.

### PUNK ROCK CATHOLICISM (AKA TATTOOS)

1. Veronica Giuliani, *Il Diario*, compiled by Maria Teresa Carloni (Siena, Italy: Edizioni Cantagalli, 2010), I, 897.

### HUMAN FORMATION FOR EVERY CATHOLIC

1. Athanasius, *On the Incarnation of the Word*, 54, 3: PG 25, 192B.

### I'VE GOT THAT GRIEF, GRIEF, GRIEF, GRIEF DOWN IN MY HEART

1. United States Conference of Catholic Bishops, "Prayer in Times of Suffering and Need," http://www.usccb.org/prayer-and-worship/prayers-and-devotions/prayers/prayer-in-times-of-suffering-and-need.cfm.

## CATHOLIC FEMINISM (AKA THINGS POPES SAID THAT NO ONE TALKS ABOUT)

1. John Paul II, *Evangelium Vitae*, 99, http://w2.vatican.va/content/john-paul-ii/en/encyclicals/documents/hf_jp-ii_enc_25031995_evangelium-vitae.html.

2. John XXIII, *Pacem in Terris*, 41, http://w2.vatican.va/content/john-xxiii/en/encyclicals/documents/hf_j-xxiii_enc_11041963_pacem.html.

3. Benedict XVI, World Day of Peace Message, January 1, 2007, 7, https://w2.vatican.va/content/benedict-xvi/en/messages/peace/documents/hf_ben-xvi_mes_20061208_xl-world-day-peace.html.

## THE EARLY CHURCH WAS THE CATHOLIC CHURCH

1. Justin Martyr, *The First Apology of Justin Martyr: Addressed to the Emperor Antonius Pius*, preface by John Kaye (London: Griffith, Farran, Okeden and Welsh, 1889).

## YOU MUST WAIT THREE DAYS TO SEE THE POPE

1. T. Oestereich, "Pope St. Gregory VII," *The Catholic Encyclopedia* (New York: Robert Appleton Company, 1909). Retrieved April 1, 2019, from *New Advent*: http://www.newadvent.org/cathen/06791c.htm.

2. Oestereich, "Pope St. Gregory VII," *The Catholic Encyclopedia*.

3. Oestereich, "Pope St. Gregory VII," *The Catholic Encyclopedia*.

4. Benedict XVI, Homily, April 24, 2005, https://w2.vatican.va/content/benedict-xvi/en/homilies/2005/documents/hf_ben-xvi_hom_20050424_inizio-pontificato.html.

## SOCIAL JUSTICE IN EVERY SIP

1. Dorothy Day, *The Long Loneliness: The Autobiography of Dorothy Day* (San Francisco: Harper and Row, 1981).

2. Dorothy Day, "Poverty and Pacifism," *The Catholic Worker*, December 1944, 1, 7.

3. Dorothy Day, "Poverty and Pacifism," *The Catholic Worker*.

## GETTING INTO THE SPIRIT OF MICHAELMAS

1. Meredith Gould, *The Catholic Home*, updated edition (New York: Image, 2006).

## SERVANT ROYALTY

1. Basil the Great, *Homily on the Saying of the Gospel according to Luke*, "I will pull down my barns and build bigger ones," and on Greed, §7 (PG 31, 276B–277A).

## PART 3: LIVING WITH LOVE

1. John of the Cross, *Sayings of Light and Love*, 64, as quoted in https://catholic-link.org/judged-love-alone.

## HIPSTER MOM: WORKING CATHOLIC MOM OF NINE

1. Zélie and Louis Martin, *A Call to a Deeper Love* (New York: Alba House, 2011), 23.

2. Hélène Mongin, *The Extraordinary Parents of St. Thérèse of Lisieux: Sts. Louis and Zélie Martin* (Huntington, IN: Our Sunday Visitor, 2015), 112.

3. Zélie and Louis Martin, *A Call to a Deeper Love*, 101.

4. Zélie and Louis Martin, *A Call to a Deeper Love*, 102.

5. Zélie and Louis Martin, *A Call to a Deeper Love*, 102.

6. "The Martin Sisters: Sisters of St. Therese," St. Therese Church, April 10, 2019, http://www.sttheresechurchalhambra.org/?DivisionID=10357&DepartmentID=22314.

## THE CATHOLIC WORKER ETHIC

1. Day, *The Long Loneliness*, 60.

2. James Martin, S.J., "Don't Call Me a Saint?" *America*, November 14, 2012, https://www.americamagazine.org/content/all-things/dont-call-me-saint.

3. The Dorothy Day Guild, "Ask in Prayer," April 10, 2019, http://dorothydayguild.org/support/petition-in-prayer.

## I'M NOT A REGULAR CATHOLIC; I'M A COOL (AND PRIDEFUL) CATHOLIC

1. Maria Faustina Kowalska, *Diary: Divine Mercy in My Soul*, 3rd ed. (Stockbridge, MA: Marian Press, 2005).

2. *Letters of Saint Augustine*, trans. John Leinenweber (Tarrytown, NY: Triumph Books, 1992), 101.

3. *Letters of Saint Augustine*, Letter 118.

4. Tommy Tighe (@theghissilent), author biography, Twitter.

## THE CATHOLIC IDEA THAT'S KEY TO GENDER EQUALITY

1. Claire Cain Miller, "Children Hurt Women's Earnings, but Not Men's (Even in Scandinavia)," *New York Times*, February 5, 2018, https://www.nytimes.com/2018/02/05/upshot/even-in-family-friendly-scandinavia-mothers-are-paid-less.amp.html.

2. Emily McCarter and Lucille Sherman, "U.S. Is Only Developed Nation without Mandated Paid Maternity Leave," Politifact Missouri, September 28, 2017, https://www.politifact.com/missouri/statements/2017/sep/28/claire-mccaskill/us-only-developed-nation-without-mandated-paid-mat.

## HOW TO MAKE A FLANNERY O'CONNOR PILGRIMAGE

1. Flannery O'Connor, *A Prayer Journal* (New York: Farrar, Straus and Giroux, 2013).

## CATHOLIC BEES

1. Catherine Croisette, "The Bee, a Symbol of the Church," Tradition in Action, April 10, 2019, https://www.traditioninaction.org/religious/f018rp_Bees_Kitt.htm.
2. Translated by Most Reverend J. H. Schlarman, Bishop of Peoria.

## CO-CREATING WITH GOD

1. Flannery O'Connor, *A Prayer Journal*.
2. Catherine of Bologna, *The Seven Spiritual Weapons* (Eugene, OR: Wipf and Stock, 2011).
3. Benedict XVI, General Audience, December 29, 2010, https://w2.vatican.va/content/benedict-xvi/en/audiences/2010/documents/hf_ben-xvi_aud_20101229.html.

## MAKING ALL THINGS NEW

1. Joseph Ratzinger, *Jesus of Nazareth: From the Baptism in the Jordan to the Transfiguration* (New York: Doubleday, 2007), 175–176.
2. Bob Schuchts, *Be Healed* (Notre Dame, IN: Ave Maria Press, 2014), 8. Emphasis added.

# ABOUT THE CONTRIBUTORS

**Kaitlyn Facista** is a Catholic convert, wife, mama, and hobbit at heart. She lives with her husband and three children in Indiana, where she can almost always be found with an iced latte in her hand and a baby on her hip. She is the creator of Tea with Tolkien, a website and online shop devoted to sharing the works and Catholic faith of J. R. R. Tolkien with the world. You can find her on Twitter at @teawithtolkien or read her blog at www.teawithtolkien.com.

**Fr. Damian Ference** is a priest of the Diocese of Cleveland and a doctoral student at the Pontifical University of St. Thomas in Rome, Italy. He is the author of *The Strangeness of Truth: Vibrant Faith in a Dark World* (Pauline Books and Media, 2019), he writes for *Word on Fire,* and he is a lifetime member of the Flannery O'Connor Society. You can find him on Twitter and Instagram as @frference.

**Jackie Francois Angel** is a wife to one swell theology teacher and a mom to three sweet, yet crazy tyrants—ahem, toddlers. She is a singer/songwriter, speaker, and author from Orange County, California, who loves Jesus, food, renovating her '80s home, and pretending that life is a musical (to her children's delight/chagrin). You can find her on Twitter and IG as @Jackiefrancois.

**Sr. Brittany Harrison, F.M.A.**, is a Salesian Sister of St. John Bosco, experienced theology teacher, and social media maven. Her writings have been featured in *Catechist* magazine and *Catholic Digest.* She is a regular contributor on Relevant Radio, sharing about youth

205

culture and Salesian spirituality. You can find her as @SisterB24 on Twitter and Instagram.

**Julie Lai** is a twenty-something young adult living in San Diego, California. She's a social media manager, writer, clinical psychology student, and big advocate for dancing even if you suck at it. You can find her on Instagram @julielai.

**Patrick Neve** is a cohost of *The Crunch* podcast and a graduate of Franciscan University. His hobbies include baseball and pretending to like IPAs.

**Samantha Povlock** is the founder of FemCatholic.com, a media platform working to reconcile Catholicism and feminism. By day she works in project management in downtown Chicago. Samantha is married to her Notre Dame college sweetheart, Matt, and they have two children.

**Katie Prejean McGrady** is the author of *Room 24: Adventures of a New Evangelist* and *Follow: Your Lifelong Adventure with Jesus*. She is an international Catholic speaker, is a (self-proclaimed) prolific Tweeter, posts way too many pictures of her daughter, Rose, on Instagram, and hosts *The Electric Waffle* podcast with her husband, Tommy.

**Matthew Sewell** is the host of *The Popecast* (@thepopecast) and the author of the popular *Popes in a Year* daily email series. By day he works at Flocknote to help parishes and dioceses build a more connected Church. He's also on Twitter more than he should be, where you can find him @matthewjsewell. Matthew, his wife (Rachel), and their firstborn (Leo) make their home in Spokane, Washington.

**Haley Stewart** is a beekeeper's wife, mom of four, writer, and speaker. Her book, *The Grace of Enough: Pursuing Less and Living More in a Throwaway Culture*, released in 2018. You can find her at her blog, *Carrots for Michaelmas*, the *Fountains of Carrots* podcast, or Instagram and Twitter, where she's @haleycarrots.

**Holly Vaughan** is a Catholic convert (class of 2014), a wife and mother to two boys, a Benedictine oblate, a theology student, and a pastoral assistant. She loves books, ink pens, and the rare opportunity to sleep. You can find her writing at http://thecatholichipster. blogspot.com.

**Theresa Zoe Williams** is a freelance writer with bylines at EpicPew and the *National Catholic Register*, among others. A quote that accurately sums up her life is "You shall know the truth and the truth shall make you odd" (Flannery O'Connor). She is a wife and mother to a couple of spunky children, and her style has been described as "neo-grunge hippie punk." She is Pennsylvanian by birth, Californian by heart, and in Colorado for the time being. You can find her on Twitter @TheresaZoe, on Instagram @TheresaZoeWilliams, or on Facebook @TheresaWilliamsWriter. She blogs at PrincipessaMeetsWorld.com.